Clifford

Happy Trails!
Nancy J Bailey
Sept 2002

Clifford

of Drummond Island

Nancy J. Bailey

Writers Club Press
San Jose New York Lincoln Shanghai

Clifford
of Drummond Island

Writers Club Press
an imprint of iUniverse.com, Inc.

For information address:
iUniverse.com, Inc.
5220 S 16th, Ste. 200
Lincoln, NE 68512
www.iuniverse.com

ISBN: 0-595-17950-9

Printed in the United States of America

For Dad.
And for all others ever loved by a horse.

LIST OF ILLUSTRATIONS

PREFACE

During the night I had a vision
—and there before me was a man riding a red horse!
He was standing among the myrtle trees in a ravine.
Behind him were red, brown and white horses.

I asked, "What are these, my lord?"

The angel who was talking with me answered,
"I will show you what they are."

Then the man standing among the myrtle trees explained,
"They are the ones the Lord has sent to go throughout the earth."

And they reported to the angel of the Lord,
who was standing among the myrtle trees,
"We have gone throughout the earth and found the whole world
at rest and in peace."

—Zechariah 1:8-11

ACKNOWLEDGEMENTS

To my loyal friend and companion, Trail Ridge Reva, CD, CGC, who has taken care of Clifford and me all these years. Thanks for running the miles with me.

Thank you to Sharon Harper, of Kerry Morgans in Forreston, Illinois, who had the insight and generosity to sell me the inimitable Clifford at a time when I needed him the most. Thank you, of course, for entrusting me with Trudy also. I am blessed with them both, and with your friendship.

Thanks to my family and friends who have tolerated the various exploits of Clifford and me.

Rhonda, thanks for being such a great "horse pal". Maybe someday I'll get over my simmering jealousy that you got to feed Secretariat a peppermint.

With love and gratitude to Carrie, who is still on her pedestal, for helping me prioritize writing this book.

Gina and Logan Hyatt, thanks for the part you played in introducing me to this very special breed.

Thanks to my friends on the Morganlist who have endured my many Clifford stories.

With gratitude to the citizens of Drummond Island, Michigan, for always making it easy to come home.

Thank you to Tess and Alan Hoey, for helping me so much with Clifford and for the wonderful trail rides!

Big thanks to Jerry Koszednar of Ann Arbor Dog Training Club, who first introduced me to the clicker method in 1994.

Thank you Jerry Page for the excellent advice.

With love and thanks to my cousin Mary Jo for the wonderful saddle that fits a Morgan so well, and for your encouragement.

To Scorch, Cajey and Piper, big hugs and kisses.

And special thanks to my heavenly Father, from whom horses and all other good things come.

CHAPTER ONE

"My beautiful, my beautiful!
That standest meekly by,
With thy proudly-arched and glossy neck,
And dark and fiery eye!"
—*Caroline Sheridan Norton (1808-1877)*

It was a mission only a horse person would understand. Driving six hours in a car, all the way to Rockford, Illinois, when there were plenty of Morgans in Michigan, might have made no sense to some people. Indeed, I had "shopped" around Michigan, surveying countless equines, their soft muzzles, their sharp sweet horsy smell, their wispy manes and eyelashes. I looked at legs and feet, disposition and movement, all the while never finding the intangible Something which fueled my search.

As I watched the cornfields rolling past, I pictured my first Morgan, Sharolyn, with her bittersweet coat and cresty neck, and her gentle, walnut eyes. I leaned back in my seat and remembered with gratitude and sadness this mare who had introduced me to Morgans, and horses in general.

Thirty years I had waited. Thirty years of dreaming; of countless horse drawings, paintings; dreams of velvet skin stretching over bone and sinew and muscle; of riding like a prairie fire with the wind in my face. Despite my fantasies, though, I knew I was green, green, green. I needed a horse that could teach me everything. I'd decided right away on a Morgan, because I liked their reputation for versatility and I figured a Morgan would have the temperament to endure my beginner's mistakes.

It was February 1994, and to my surprise, when I started looking, I saw a lot of horses that didn't look like Morgans to me. They were beautiful,

1

but tall and rangy. Most of them were missing something. I wanted a horse like Figure, the original Morgan stallion who had started the breed back in the 1700s.

Figure had been bay, and according to legend was short and sturdy. He'd belonged to a New England schoolmaster named Justin Morgan. The horse was ridiculed by many because of his size. But he could work all day hauling logs in the rocky terrain of Vermont lumber camps, then go into town at night and win races. He competed with thoroughbreds and all kinds of other horses that had been bred for speed, and he won every race he ever ran. He was reputed to be a powerful stallion with a gentle and kind disposition. His most distinctive characteristic, though, was his ability to reproduce his own traits. Every mare he was bred to went on to produce a foal that was a carbon copy of himself.

I loved the story of Figure; loved the fact that the Morgan was the first breed of horse produced in America.

During my search for a Figure of my own, I finally was referred to Kelly Batton. She was giving lessons at a barn in South Lyon, which her mother had sold to new owners. I didn't realize it at the time, but Batton's Farm was legendary in Michigan, and now a crumbling dynasty of old Morgan bloodlines.

Kelly told me about a mare that was for sale, and invited me to come and start taking lessons there. That way, even if I didn't like the mare, I could learn to ride on Morgans. This seemed like a great idea!

I was in the middle of my first lesson, bouncing along the rail on an old mare named Cinnamon, when someone led a black horse into the arena.

"Nancy," Kelly said, "This is Sharolyn."

The next few moments were like a dream. The girl got on this equine vision, and proceeded to ride her around the arena. That horse, Batton's Sharolyn, stood like a carved ebony chess piece, then suddenly exploded into motion. Her knees and hocks flew up in the air and she arched her neck and pranced and snorted. Because I was an artist, I knew she appealed to my esthetic senses. But there was something more. Angels sang when I looked at her. That horse wasn't just pretty. She twinkled. She shimmered.

I later learned that Sharolyn was sired by JJ's Monarch, out of a mare named Highover Coralyn. Sharolyn had been bred in Illinois, by Sharon Harper of Kerry Morgans. But Coralyn, her dam, was sold to Battons and brought to Michigan before she was born. Sharolyn was nine years old, and seal brown, not black, but her winter coat was very dark. And she was my horse—it was like I had known her in a past life or something, and had been looking for her. Even more strangely, it was like she knew me too.

A couple by the name of Jerry and Sue Page had owned her since she was a weanling. They'd decided to sell her because they weren't spending enough time with her. She had earned a reputation for being hot and difficult, which I resented, because that was not true at all. She moved high, was snorty and proud and sensitive, but she had perfect ground manners. She was bright, patient, willing and wonderful. She stood still when the saddle slid underneath her belly because I didn't tighten the cinch enough. She stopped and waited for me when I fell off. She took carrots gently from my hands. She nickered to me when I arrived.

Though I had always loved horses, I'd harbored a notion that they liked to eat, and weren't much interested in anything else. I had never been around horse people much, or known a horse on a personal level. I had read countless horse stories but had put them off as fanciful tales. I wasn't expecting much from horse ownership, other than a lot of one-sided affection and some great trail rides. Imagine my utter delight and infatuation when I discovered that this mare was more like a dog! That she would come to me, follow me around, nuzzle me and blow in my hair!

She was a dream come true. And she was beautiful. Very up-headed with an arched and cresty neck, she resembled a Friesian in miniature. And could she *trot!*

The Pages came to visit us a couple of times, interested in how Sharolyn and I were getting along. Jerry showed me how he had taught her to "park out", or stretch in a show pose. Sue brought me a pewter picture frame with horses engraved on it. They were kind people and I could tell Sharolyn had come from a good place.

I found myself withdrawing from the real world. I existed to ride that horse. Every morning I'd get dressed in my riding clothes while my German shepherd, Reva, would whine and groan with excitement. She'd ride out to the barn with me. She'd wait while I saddled Sharolyn, then I'd say, "Reva, go get my helmet."

Reva would go flying out of the barn. She'd leap into the back of my pickup, a red Sonoma dubbed the "Revabus". She would grab my helmet and bring it in to me, holding it high with the straps swinging down.

We'd be gone all day. The world consisted of Reva and Sharolyn and me.

A few weeks after I bought her, I moved Sharolyn to a different barn where she and I could go out and trail ride. When Kelly loaded her into the trailer, she said, "This horse won't go on the trails. She hasn't been out of the arena enough; she's only been on the roads a few times in her life. Be careful."

Our first ride took us on a trail through the back of the property, walking among the trees, swishing through piles of wet brown leaves. Sharolyn's head was high, and she smelled the air, blowing a little snort with every breath. Reva trotted by Sharolyn's right rear leg, occasionally breaking off to investigate some odor in the damp ground, then returning to her position.

We rode for hours that day, through woods and fields, along the river, walking through the mud and the hushed brown grass of early spring.

Each day we explored the vast state trails, scaring up birds and brushing past budding twigs. One afternoon, my husband Bruce came with us, walking behind the horse. We had gone a couple of miles when the path rose abruptly, running up a long, steep hill. The trees at the top towered far above us.

"It would be easiest for you if you'd just grab her tail," I called. "She'll pull you right up there."

"She might kick me," he said.

I shrugged and rode on. To my knowledge, she had never kicked anyone, and never would. Reva remained in position with the mare, and we trotted up together, leaving Bruce to struggle up on his own. At the top, without my bidding, Sharolyn stopped and turned her head to look back.

I gasped. "She's waiting for you!"

She did that for the rest of the afternoon. Every time he fell behind, she knew it, and she would stop and look back, waiting patiently for him to catch up.

I was spending hours with my new friend every day; brushing her, combing her mane and talking to her, feeding her carrots and apples and smelling her sweet smell. She would greet Reva and me when we arrived, and was always willing and eager to do whatever I felt like doing. I imagined taking her to Morgan shows, and had fantasies of all the future ribbons we would win in the English Pleasure classes. I needed to learn how to ride saddle seat! And I couldn't believe she had never been bred. I envisioned a little Sharolyn baby, high stepping and up-headed and snorty; a carbon copy of its dam.

People gushed over her. I would meet other riders on the trails, and they would literally stop to stare as we went charging past. "She is awesome!" they would say. "Look at her move!"

Then one day, she was a little lame in her hind legs. I didn't ride that day, thinking she must be sore from all the activity. The next day, she was no better, and I called the vet. He got out of his truck, took one look at her, and said, "This mare has E.P.M."

"What?"

"Equine protozoal myeloencephalitis. A parasite has gotten into her bloodstream and munched through her nervous system."

"A parasite?"

"There's no preventative. They think it is spread through bird stools. It affects some horses, not all of them."

I had never heard of such a thing. This couldn't happen to us. Surely she was just a little sore, and she would be fine in a few days.

But she worsened. Despite our treatments, she was wobbly, stumbling as her hips swayed and listed dangerously, first in one direction, then the other. Five days after her diagnosis, she was down and couldn't get up. The next day, she could not raise her head.

That day, when I walked into the barn, I had my friends Rita and Gina with me. All was still, and as we entered the aisle, Rita said, "Where is she?"

"Down at the end, there." When I answered, I heard Sharolyn begin thrashing violently in her stall at the sound of my voice. It was time to get up! We had places to go!

I knew at that moment that I couldn't force this mare to lie there while we tried in vain to cure her. She had too much heart; too much spirit to lie quietly waiting to die.

The stall door was open, and she lay on her side rolling her eye back, trying to see out. I went in and sat down next to her. Her nostrils flared, blowing shavings across the floor. I began stroking her smooth, warm neck. "Don't worry, Sharolyn."

Her eyes softened, and I could feel her begin to relax as I spoke to her. I took a deep breath, and explained to her that she would have to go on ahead for a little while; but that she would be able to run and play. I said I'd be along someday and we would do great things when we met again. I didn't cry, because I knew she would sense my emotions and it would upset her. Dr. Cawley came in and injected her quickly, and I sat there with her as she died.

I had owned Sharolyn for eight beautiful weeks. I have never forgotten the lesson she taught me—that horses are as capable of love as we are—and how they will blossom if someone believes in them.

I didn't expect the colossal grief that followed her death. I could not sleep. I could not eat. I would just sit and stare out the window, while Reva sat with her head in my lap.

One day I had a phone call from a woman inquiring about art work. She let slip that she had owned horses for years. I suddenly found myself pouring my heart out to this person I barely knew. "I don't know what's the matter with me. I can't function. I've lost pets before, but never like this. I lost a human friend once, and this is actually closer to that experience."

She sighed. "When you lose a horse, you lose a part of yourself. It's because you become physically one with that animal. It links you in a different way."

I pictured myself as a centaur, the mythical creature; half man, half horse. Despite the bizarre imagery, I realized that in a way this was really true. I hadn't owned her for long, but during our many hours together, Sharolyn and I had become physically and spiritually linked.

Sue Page called me, saying Jerry was out of the country but he would call me when he got back. "I'm so sorry," she said. "It's so unfair that you would lose her right after you bought her."

"I'd do it all over again," I said.

When Jerry did call a few days later, the first thing he said was, "I want you to get another horse right away."

His voice triggered something in me, and I immediately began to sob, uncontrollably and embarrassingly, into the phone. "Oh, no, Jerry. I just can't."

"Yes. Make yourself do it, right away. Because if you don't, you'll make a martyr out of her, and you'll never own another horse. And someone like you should have a horse."

At first I couldn't even consider his suggestion. The thought of replacing Sharolyn seemed like a betrayal, a dishonor to her memory and the bond we had shared. But after much agonizing deliberation, I realized that he was right. I didn't know what else to do with this terrible space that had been carved in me. Besides, Reva was depressed, having lost her new companion and the daily ride she had so fiercely loved. If I couldn't do it for myself, I could do it for her.

As I reluctantly began my search, I wondered where I'd ever find another mare like Sharolyn. It made sense to go back to the source. Her breeder, Sharon Harper, was still producing Morgans in Illinois, with the help of her daughter Shannon.

And that was what had brought me here.

Bruce turned the car off the highway, and when I saw the sign that said, "Kerry Morgans", a surprising thrill of anticipation ran down my spine. As the car rolled up the shady driveway, we were heralded with a loud equine beller. I opened the door and stepped out. The early spring air smelled like mud and new leaves. There was a big, roughened old red barn. I knew it was full of Morgans, beautiful Morgans, and for the first time in weeks, I felt a tingle of hope.

CHAPTER TWO

"Ask me to show you poetry in motion, and I will show you a horse."
—Unknown

Serendipity Aries B was nothing short of equine royalty. He marched forth from his stall with an air of benign interest, his head up, gentle eyes shining, tiny ears perked. I admired his wide chest, short back and straight legs, and the beautiful bay coloring; dark mane and tail. He stood quietly while I patted and stroked him. "Can he have a candy?"

"Well, some stallions you can't do that with," Shannon said. "But he's okay."

He took the peppermint from my hand, his lips barely whispering across my palm.

He was obviously very attached to Sharon. Though I had given him the candy, he didn't beg for more, content instead to stand quietly by her side. Sharon was tiny and stout, with a face weathered by things unknown. Her expression was reminiscent of someone who might have crossed the prairie in a covered wagon, enduring hardships and wind and sun. Her hair was like a thatch of straw across her forehead. Her shoulders were square, her arms thick and capable. Her roughened hands ran gently along the horse's neck. "He's twenty years old," she smiled proudly.

"You're kidding!" I stepped back, searching the regal stallion for signs of graying, a sag in the backbone, anything.

Just then, a loud clatter sounded from the row of stalls. I looked up to see a blazed face peering over the top of the stall wall.

"Get down!" Shannon and Sharon shouted in unison.

The face disappeared.

"Who was that?"

Sharon smiled. "We'll save him for last. I'll show you the mares now."

My heart ached to look at them. Each one was so lovely, and so obviously pure Morgan. They came out of the stalls like lambs, but when Sharon turned them loose in the paddock, each became a creature of the air, a dancing, leaping vision, trotting to a silent beat and snorting like a locomotive. Aries B had produced a number of daughters with the Kerry mares, all of which had wonderful creative names honoring their sire: Kerry Ariel, Kerry Arabella, Kerry Aria. Each one had the bay coloring, the high light motion, and the sweet disposition of Aries B.

Kerry Xcaliber, a yearling colt also sired by Aries, was led into the arena and released. He was the picture of rhythm floating above the earth, his short black mane blowing, his tail waving high. Even at this young age he was muscled and looked powerful and masculine, yet his legs were refined and elegant, his dished face sweet, with an innocent expression. I could imagine that this must have been close to how the original Morgan, Figure, looked at that age. Shannon was shaking a milk jug that had some gravel in it. The rattling spurred on the little colt's movement. Finally, she called, "Cal!"

He stopped and looked at her with his ears up.

"Cal! Come here!" she coaxed. But she was shaking the jug, rattling the stones while she called. He stood with his long front legs thrust forward, leaning back hesitantly, an exquisite picture of indecision.

Sharon laughed, took him by the halter and led him back inside. I hated to see him go. I felt I could have watched him for hours.

Then Sharon came out leading a dark bay mare, with a filly trotting closely by her side. "Here's Kerry Hallelujah."

"Oh!" I exclaimed. This was mare I had most wanted to see, because she was a daughter of Sharolyn's full sister. But any fantasies I'd had about Hallelujah dissolved when I saw that filly. The newest daughter of Aries B, Kerry Airatude was four weeks old, with a soft fuzzy coat, the eyes of a fawn, and legs that went on and on. She trotted next to her mother with knees and hocks that flung themselves skyward. Her tail stood straight up, and her tiny hooves never seemed to touch the ground. I was smitten.

The pair was led away too soon. My head was swimming with visions of beautiful bay Morgans; their black manes and tails blowing, their black legs and hooves flashing in movement.

Then Sharon approached the stall where the ruckus was coming from. "This is Buckets."

"Buckets?"

"Yes. His mother had no milk when he was born, and he was bucket-fed for the first few days of his life."

Buckets had obviously never been properly weaned. He thrust his nose out eagerly, snuffling me, searching for goodies. Sharon stepped over to him and held up a warning finger. "Thump, thump," his lips snapped together. She slid the stall door open and hooked the lead rope onto his halter.

He stepped lightly out next to her, a shining red chestnut with his blazed face pointed curiously in my direction. "It was a little hard getting used to all that white on his face," Sharon said. "Most of our Morgans have little or no white."

I followed her outside, carrying the camera. I thought the least I could do was take a video of this young gelding that she obviously wanted to sell. He walked quietly with her to the outdoor arena. His flanks gleamed red in the sun, and his long yellow mane was a mass of disheveled curls. She closed the gate behind her and unhooked him. She clucked to him softly, and he trotted in a circle. He moved lightly and freely like the rest of her Morgans, arching his long neck proudly, purring happy snorts. But he was not overly cooperative about showing off. He was quite intrigued by the camera and kept coming over to stick his face in it.

"He's friendly," I said.

"Oh yeah," her reply was casual, offhand. It soon turned out that 'friendly' was an understatement. Taking pictures of Buckets was an exercise in the Macro sense of the word. I got pictures of his nostril, pictures of his whiskers and the white diamond on the end of his nose. I got a good shot of his leering, rolling eye as he shook his mane wickedly and spun away.

Hoping to impress me further, Sharon led Buckets out and put him in a bitting rig; the straps and buckles running across his chest and around his girth like a harness. She fed him peppermints as he stood in the cross ties, which he crunched greedily. She then led him off and proceeded to longe him around the arena. I continued to film. I had to admit that he was very cute with his blinkers on. His neck arched prettily, his hocks moved high.

"What's his registered name?" I asked.

"Kerry B Proud. His sire is Serendipity Aries B, his dam is Kerry Pride 'N Joy."

I could see how the name worked out. Aries B + Pride 'N Joy = B Proud. And it was fitting. The little horse was obviously full of himself.

Still, I could not get the high-stepping filly out of my mind. I knew she was going to be another Sharolyn. After Buckets was put away, I followed Sharon into her house to look at papers, and then spent the next hour begging her to sell me that filly.

"Do you want her shown? I'll show her!" I wheedled.

"She'd probably fit in your trunk, Nancy," Shannon said laughingly.

I didn't mind the fact that Airatude was a baby. I knew she was supposed to be my horse. But Sharon was firm. Those Aries B daughters were not for sale. No way, no how.

Sadly, I followed her back out to the barn while she did the evening feeding. I walked over to Buckets' stall and looked in at him. He thrust his nose out and thumped his lips at me. I looked at his long mane, which hung down over his eyes. He was chestnut—not what I wanted. He was a gelding—not what I wanted. He was a two-year-old—probably not what I could handle. I hadn't imagined giving up my dream of an elegant bay mare, especially for a mouthy chestnut colt named Buckets. But I needed a horse. He was a son of that wonderful stallion, Aries B. His dam was related to Sharolyn. And anyway, maybe it was better to get something different than the mare I still mourned. If I came home with a mare or filly, maybe my expectations would be too high.

"Okay," I said. "I'll take him."

CHAPTER THREE

"I can always tell which is the front end of a horse, but beyond that,
my art is not above the ordinary."
—Mark Twain

We hauled Buckets from Rockford Illinois, back to Marshfire Farm in Saline, Michigan, through a June rainstorm. He had leaped into the trailer after a brief hesitation, and was rewarded with peppermints. When he backed out of the trailer, he bellered at the other horses. Steeped in hay, they didn't answer.

Marshfire Farm was a Morgan farm owned by my friends Gina and Logan Hyatt. It was a comfortable place, the barn surrounded by huge weeping willow trees and ducks floating contentedly on a deep rippling pond. I led Buckets into the arena on the longe line and clucked to him. He stepped right out, trotting jauntily and swishing his tail, his eyes gleaming with excitement.

"Let's see how tall he is," Logan said. He walked up to Buckets with a tape. Buckets reached for the tape and Logan pulled it back. I grabbed him by the halter.

"He's thirteen two," Logan said, smiling. "Well, he'll probably grow. They can grow until they're five. He sure has a beautiful head and throat."

I beamed. We put Buckets in the cross ties and I began brushing him. Logan got out the Show Sheen and polished his coat until he gleamed like a new penny.

The next day, I decided to longe him outside. I brought my sister Rebecca to the farm with me, and instructed her to take pictures. She did. She took pictures of Buckets galloping and screaming while I spun desperately in the middle of the circle. She took pictures of Buckets getting tangled up in the longe line. She took pictures of Buckets running away while I chased him.

Due to my dog training background, I had enough sense to know that I couldn't end a lesson this way. I asked him to walk nicely, in one complete circle. I shortened the line. He was excited and nervous, and it took a good half hour before he did it. But he did it. Then we quit, and I went home exhausted.

The next day I brought Reva with me to the barn. I wanted to see how Buckets would be with dogs. He took an immediate interest in her. She stood quietly while he sniffed her all over, mouthing her gently. I knew Sharon didn't have a dog, and wondered if he had ever seen one. He was in the cross ties, but I was worried he would bite her, because he was so mouthy. I watched closely, but he was gentle. Finally, he grabbed her ear and pulled. I held my breath, but Reva did nothing. He must have been using only his lips. I decided that was enough experimentation, though, and told Reva to move off, which she did. Buckets watched her go, nodding his head.

"You're smart not to start trouble with her. She's almost as big as you."

I paused, looking at him. "You know, you remind me of my Great Uncle, Clifford. He was a short little guy, and he would have pulled her ears too. He was a tease."

In fact, in his younger days, Uncle Clifford had been a redhead. His descendants, which now populated Drummond Island with alarming prolificacy, were redheads too. Despite the reputation this hair color had earned, Uncle Clifford had a sweet side. I remembered his protests when Aunt Connie had grounded cousin Anne and me on a summer afternoon.

"Connie," he had said. "Why don't you let those girls go down and ride Frank's ponies? Don't make them stay here and sit around the house!"

He had scored big points with me that day. We did go ride the black ponies, bareback, squeezing their fat, sun-warmed sides between our knees and galloping through the grass with the wind in our hair. It was one of my few precious childhood memories that included horses, and I owed it to Uncle Clifford.

When I put Buckets back in his stall, he thumped the feed bin impatiently. "Yeah," I said. "Uncle Clifford liked grain, too. Of course, he preferred a different variety."

From that point on, Buckets had a new name.

The next day, I reviewed my Linda Tellington-Jones video, and decided that Buckets, now Clifford, needed to learn about personal space. On my way to the farm, I went to the feed store and bought a short whip. I brought Clifford outside. I began touching him with the whip, running it all over his body to get him accustomed to the feel of it. I treated the whip as an extension of my hand, as Tellington-Jones had advised. I wanted to teach him that a tap on the croup meant, "step forward", a tap on the chest meant, "stop".

He looked around at rocks and bushes with his head high and snorting. Every tree was a monster, every blowing leaf a predatory threat. He kept jumping on top of me, expecting me to protect him. Every time he bumped me, or got too close, I swatted him with the whip. One time, after smacking him, I gave him too much slack on the lead rope, and his heels shot past my skull. A moment later, his jitters caused him to jump forward onto my foot.

Round and round we went; me brandishing that whip, and Clifford jumping and jigging.

I was soaked with sweat, frustrated and angry; with myself more than the colt. I put him back in his stall, sat down on a hay bale, and cried. How I missed Sharolyn! She would have never done this! I was foolish to buy such a green horse, when I myself was so inexperienced. Besides, he wasn't at all what I wanted. What a stupid choice I had made!

I walked up to the house to get a drink of water, while Gina listened sympathetically to my woes. "Come on down and help me feed," she said. "Take your mind off it. You'll feel better."

As I moved from stall to stall with flakes of hay, speaking softly to each horse and listening to their hollow crunching, I did feel calmer. But I still had a nagging ache that perhaps I had done the wrong thing, made the wrong choice; and of course there was the sadness of knowing that Sharolyn was never coming back. I could never replace her.

Finished with the evening feed, Gina and I walked slowly up the barn aisle. "You just need to give him time," she said.

She went over to the front of Clifford's stall and looked in. He stood with his head in the corner, munching hay contentedly. "He's still a baby. And the nice thing about buying the wrong horse is, even if he isn't right for you, it's a learning experience. You can always sell him later."

I stepped over to stand beside her. "Learning experience is right."

At the sound of my voice, up popped the colt's head. His eyes brightened. He walked over to me immediately, stuck his head out and began mouthing my shoulder. I smiled, and then as he continued to bump and nuzzle me, I started laughing. He knew me! He liked me! He forgave me!

Despite my ineptitude, the little red Morgan was making it very clear that everything was going to be all right.

CHAPTER FOUR

"Anything forced and misunderstood can never be beautiful."
—*Xenophon (400 B.C.)*

"He's too small for you. He's a kid's horse," my sister Raechel said, surveying Clifford with authority. "Look at those front legs. Look at how he toes out. He'll never be a performance horse. He's cute, but you need to sell him and get yourself something else."

I regarded the little horse ruefully. "You don't think he'll grow?"

"He might grow, a little. But he's a kid's horse. He's cute though."

She had ridden endurance for years, and her Arabian mare had been awarded a five thousand mile medallion. Raechel lived in Utah, which was a long way from Michigan, so she'd had no input on my selection. When she'd first heard that I was horse shopping, she had sent me a big box of old "Equus" magazines. They'd been packed with information, which I had absorbed greedily, and then I'd subscribed to the magazine.

"You should have gotten an Arab. I could have helped you find a good one," she said.

"Well, I chose Morgans because they were supposed to be gentle and good with greenhorns like me. I was perhaps misinformed, but I thought an Arab might be too much for me to handle."

"But he's green too! You must have heard that old saying, 'Green plus green equals black and blue!'"

I had heard it. I was no horse expert, that was for sure. I had in fact resorted to my dog training methods to work with Clifford. I was a clicker trainer, employing a technique that had been used by dolphin trainers for years, but at the time was just catching on in the dog-training world. It involved the use of a small plastic toy, which, when squeezed, made a clicking sound. The animal learned that the sound of the click meant food was coming. It was therefore a sound which communicated, "Yes!" to the animal, at the moment a desired behavior occurred. It increased the chances of the behavior occurring again. Best of all, it made training humane, easy and fun.

At that time I'd never heard of anyone using a clicker on a horse, but he was certainly food motivated. He gladly worked for peppermints, or cut-up pieces of carrots or apples. I clicked him for putting his head in his halter, clicked him for giving me my space, clicked him for yielding to pressure. Combined with what I had learned from my Tellington-Jones tape, it seemed to be working out all right. Clifford got so that when he heard the click, he would immediately swing his head around and look for the treat. He was an eager and willing student. He certainly didn't seem to mind that I used the method on my dogs too.

So, I treated Clifford much as if he were a puppy. And I knew one of the important things about raising puppies is socialization. It seemed sensible to trailer him as much as possible, expose him to as much as I could. So I'd hauled him the six hours to the Upper Peninsula. This was after many adventures in hauling downstate. If they'd allowed horses in shopping malls, I would undoubtedly have done that too.

Clifford was busy cropping grass while I held the end of his longe line. He paid no attention to Raechel's scrutiny. There was plenty of new clover at our campsite on Drummond Island, which until now had been horse-free. It was a green, sun-dappled clearing in the woods. At the top of the gradual slope of grass, a small camper hunkered. Attached to it was a wooden deck that my Dad had built a few years prior, and we would sit there in the evenings when shadows grew long, and listen to the loons call from the distant inland lakes. A dirt road meandered past, winding its way through the thick stands of cedar, spruce and birch.

Clifford snorted happily, blowing into the clover. Raechel's words made me think of what had recently happened at a trail ride down at

Waterloo Recreation Area. I had brought Clifford to the gathering, thinking it would be good for him. He was still too young to ride, but I could lead him around, at least.

When I had unloaded him from the trailer, I'd heard a raspy voice shouting, "What is that? Hey, what is that thang?"

I paid it no heed. I was tying Clifford to the trailer.

"What is that thang, Hon?"

I finally realized the voice was addressing me, and I turned to see a grizzled, gray-headed man. He was astride a sleepy spotted horse as wide as a couch. He was with a group of scruffy cowboys, all sitting on horses as big as his. They leaned easily on their saddle horns, smoking cigarettes and regarding Clifford and me with crooked, gap-toothed hilarity.

"What is that?" the old man asked again.

"It's a Morgan."

"That thang looks like a greyhound dog!" he cackled. The whole group burst into loud guffaws as the old man put the spurs to his horse's massive sides and ambled away.

"He's a *baby!*" I shrieked. "He's *two years old!* And he's a *good boy!*"

But the group of them had gone up the trail, still laughing and hooting. I heard one of them mumble, "Yeah, good fer nuthin'!"

Now Raechel was telling me basically the same thing. I couldn't argue. These were the opinions of experienced horse people. What did I know?

My Dad came over, unwrapping a peppermint. Clifford, hearing the cellophane crackle, jerked his head up and walked over to Dad. He pinned his ears, swung his head and leered, thumping his lips together impatiently. Dad quickly slipped him the peppermint, which Clifford took with a gratuitous crunch.

"Ugh, you really shouldn't reward him for making those ugly faces," I said.

Dad gave the colt a pat on the shoulder. "Clifford, you're a nice horse."

"Come on Cliffy," I said. "Show Grandpa how you can trot."

We had worked and worked on longeing. The clicker had been a great help in teaching Clifford the verbal commands for different gaits, and especially for "whoa". He stepped right out to the end of the line and trotted perkily in a circle. "Walk," I said softly. He dropped to a walk. "Trot up," I said, and he burst forward, his muscles rippling, mane and tail flowing, a vision in red and gold. The sun danced on his coat, and his head was up, eyes happy, nostrils flaring and purring little snorts.

"Why, she's done a good job training him!" Raechel murmured to her husband. I pretended not to hear, but I smiled inside. Watching Clifford, I felt a sudden kinship with Justin Morgan, the schoolmaster. Back in the 1700s, he'd owned a little bay horse. That horse, too, was the object of ridicule and jokes among many horse people who thought they knew better.

CHAPTER FIVE

"Character is power."
—Booker T. Washington

I tried to teach Clifford to peg out at camp. First, I tied him up with a longe line, like a dog. He would inadvertently turn, get the line wrapped around his legs, then whirl and spin until he had himself trussed up like a calf. Plop, over he'd go. He was smart enough not to struggle when he hit the ground; he'd just wait for me to come and untangle him. Finally, we rigged up a piece of garden hose and ran a rope through it. This was successful and he learned to step over it.

But the peg line, of course, would not suffice for overnight. So every evening I trundled him over to the farm of some cousins, Tess and Alan Hoey. They owned a number of horses; some Arabians, an Appaloosa and one enormous quarter horse. Clifford was diminutive compared to the others, and it quickly became apparent that he was considered dog meat. They chased him mercilessly, striking out with quick hooves and gleaming teeth. Around the field they would go, the big horses with their ears pinned, manes flying and muscles churning, and Clifford stretched out ahead of them like a fleeing red fox. Finally they would tire of the chase, drop their heads and graze. Clifford would stand a little distance from the group, pretending to nibble the grass while he eyed them warily. After a brief respite, the thundering persecution would begin again. One day they harassed him so aggressively that he snapped right through their board fence and went galloping down the road. From that point on, he stayed by himself in an adjoining pasture, and was very content to do so.

A corral at camp was in order. Dad marked out the spot for it; that which had been my grandfather's old potato patch; a flat area by the road. The ferns had overtaken the space, and there were small poplar trees all around it.

Dad walked around in the woods and marked the trees that were to become posts and those that were to become rails. They all were cedar. When he had selected the right number of trees, he took his tractor and chainsaw, and cut them down, one by one. The sound of the chainsaw roared through the woods, making the silence heavy between cuttings. I followed him with chains, and would wrap the chain around each felled tree and then Dad would pull it out with the tractor.

"We ought to teach Clifford to skid these logs out," I gasped one day as I helped Dad move a large one into position. "That's what the first Morgan did for a living."

Bruce came up on weekends and dug post holes. This was no easy task, as the ground was riddled with rocks, many of them huge and deep. The posts themselves were of dimensions that could have contained an elephant.

Dad and I spent long afternoons stripping the logs, peeling the bark away from the gleaming white wood beneath. While we worked, he told me stories of his grandfather, George Warren Bailey, his grandmother Cornelia Edgerton, and the Bailey family. George Warren was the second white man to settle on Drummond, sailing in from Wisconsin and going on to set up seven lumber camps around the Island. He had a passel of kids, whose antics were legendary and whose many descendants still called the Island home.

Dad was an engaging storyteller, with the ability to add life to every narrative. He spoke of he and his brother and cousins playing cowboys and Indians in the woods, pegging chicken dung at each other and skinny-dipping in the bay. His tales were entertaining and often hilarious.

We had given up on keeping Clifford tied. During the construction of his corral, he roamed around camp, cropping grass. In the heat of the afternoon, the flies would begin to swarm, and he would amble across the road to the sawmill and roll in the sawdust pile. He'd come back with shavings speckling his mane, and smelling of cedar and balsam. Reva accompanied him, circling and worrying constantly.

The sawmill was an ancient, hulking monstrosity that had belonged to my grandfather. It ran on a diesel engine. It had built a number of cabins and homes over the years, and Dad and his brothers, Bob and Warren, still used it nearly daily every summer.

Near the road, by the pile of scrap lumber, Dad had placed a sign that said, "For Sale, Firewood. Leave money in the can. Cash, check, or credit card." A rusty coffee can was nailed to a board, which lay on the ground nearby. People would come out to load up the wood, and they usually left a dollar or two in the can.

One day Dad saw a truck pull up at the mill. They drove off after loading some wood. It was time for him to take a break, so he decided to walk over and check the can. When he peeled off the lid, he found a fifty-dollar bill.

He stood up and looked down the road, but the truck was long gone. He hustled over to his jeep and got in, and roared down the road after them. When he reached town, down by Four Corners, he recognized their truck sitting in the grocery store parking lot. He beeped his horn and pulled up beside it to see a pair of young women inside, both of whom were near tears.

He grinned at them amiably. "Did you lose something?"

"Yes! We lost a fifty-dollar bill! It was part of our vacation budget and now we can't eat!"

He held up the fifty. "You didn't lose it."

That was the largest lump sum that the small "firewood business" produced. No one ever did leave a credit card.

The days of summer were long and bright. My sister Rebecca would come up on weekends, toting her infant, Jacob. She was a claims adjuster and dealt with car thieves and city life all day, so enjoyed the respite of the north woods. She was, however, not necessarily an out-doorsy person. One hot afternoon, while she and Bruce and I were enjoying a cold drink, a shrill birdcall echoed from the woods north of camp. A moment later, a call to the south answered it.

"What is that noise?" Rebecca asked.

I looked at her solemnly. "Those are black bears, signaling each other. That sound is their claws, squeaking on the trees."

"Really?"

Bruce clapped a hand over his mouth and abruptly walked away.

In the heat of the afternoon, Clifford would often seek out a shady spot, lie down and rest. One day he was curled up not far from me while I sat on the deck. Dad had gone to town, and all was quiet. I was immersed in a book when suddenly a loud grunt broke my concentra-tion. I looked up and around, then heard another grunt, followed by a little squeal. I looked over and there lay Clifford with his eyes shut tight and his nose pressed into the ground. His neck arched a bit, his feet twitched, and he squeaked and groaned.

He stirred, then awakened and looked around, seeming dazed. When he finally looked up at me, I said, "So were you chasing rabbits, or what?"

The corral project went on for weeks. Mom came out one day when we had a few of the fence posts up, and were still stripping logs. Bruce was digging the last posthole. He was dripping with sweat, and dirt smudged his shirt and face.

"I don't think I want the corral here," Mom said.

Dad stopped peeling logs and stood up straight, wiping his forehead. Bruce froze in place. I saw his face, which was already flushed from exertion, transform into a deeper shade of crimson.

"It's too close to the camper. It will attract flies."

I thought Bruce was going to blow a gasket. He threw the post hole digger down and walked away.

"Well!" Dad said. "Where would you have us put it?"

I went after Bruce. He had gone up to the water pump, and was furiously cranking the pump handle. He had a small plastic cup in his hand. I watched as he drank.

"I'll take some of that," I said.

He pumped me a cupful, and I took a sip. It was ice cold, the perfect refreshment in the heat of the day.

"I cannot believe her!" he whispered. "I have been working my tail off on those post holes! Now she's telling me we have to move the corral?"

"Just wait. Dad will handle it."

We waited in silence behind the camper. After awhile Mom got in the car and drove off. Dad kept peeling.

"Your mother wants a gazebo," he told us when we got back. "She wants it in time for the reunion this summer."

That was six weeks away.

"Oh my God!" I said. "How are you gonna do that?"

He smiled. "Guess I'll have to talk to Uncle Bob."

Uncle Bob had been a builder by trade, and he showed up at the crack of dawn the next morning. Despite the eighty-degree weather, he always wore dark brown or blue work suits with long sleeves. His voice was the opposite of Dad's; mild and sort of wispy-sounding. He was always cheerful.

The two brothers went to work on that gazebo. We had set the rest of the posts in the corral, and Dad had tied tape around it to simulate an electric wire. It kept Clifford in for about an hour.

More postholes were dug around the fire pit, which was a big pile of rocks. The woods echoed with the sounds of pounding and sawing. The gazebo, from the looks of things, was going to be roughly the size of the Pontiac Silverdome. Dad and Uncle Bob worked independently of each other. Uncle Bob had brought his bright yellow portable scaffolds, which were unsettlingly wobbly, but the two men, both in their seventies, clambered up and down them without hesitation. Dad seemed to enjoy balancing on the rafters on the balls of his feet, suspended over that fire pit, while he ran the chain saw. I couldn't watch.

Clifford found the whole process fascinating. He nosed around the work area, and if he found a stray board lying anywhere, he'd pick it up and move it. Dad would beller at him from the roof.

"Clifford! Leave that alone!"

Clifford would stop, roll one eye, and continue dragging the board.

"Hey!" Dad would pound with his hammer for emphasis. "Get out of there! You'd better dangle!"

This would be the cue for Reva to jump and snap at him. Clifford would drop the board, shaking and rolling his head, and trot away with the big dog on his heels.

Once, watching the little horse flip his mane around, I had a sudden flashback to the previous Christmas. In the middle of the mass of crackling paper and the squeals of nieces and nephews, my mother presented Dad with a hat that she had made for him. It was a blue knitted cap, with tinsel around the brim, and strings with big tinfoil bells and tiny plastic animals dangling from it. There were little seals and bears and giraffes swinging from Dad's head, bobbing past his eyes and ears. While he unwrapped his gifts, Dad would flip his head this way and that, so that the tinsel sparkled and the bells and animals swung wildly around his face.

As Clifford galloped off, Bruce glanced up from where he was pounding nails. "Dad and that horse really seem to get along."

I shrugged. "Why wouldn't they? They're exactly alike!"

Dad always saw to it that the work site was free of nails, that the holes were covered, so the area was as safe as possible. He generally discouraged Clifford from hanging around there very much. But when we took breaks, he would be ready with peppermints. Clifford would seek him out, following him everywhere. If Dad pulled up a lawn chair, Clifford would go and stand behind him, swishing his tail, eyes half shut. One day, he rested his chin on Dad's head. He stood like that for awhile.

"That's getting heavy," Dad said, looking at me.

"That's because he's asleep," I said.

There he stood, snoring away, with his head getting heavier and heavier while Dad tried not to move.

The story Dad loves to recount is when he and Uncle Bob were both on hands and knees, looking down into one of the postholes. Clifford came up and lowered his head and looked down into it, too.

"I have never seen a horse behave like that one does!" Uncle Bob exclaimed.

One hot afternoon, while they were getting the roof on the gazebo, a squawk came from inside the camper, and Mom emerged. "I was in the bathroom and he was looking at me through the window!"

Dad straightened up from his bent position on the rafters. "Who?"

Unable to contain her laughter, she lifted her arm and pointed. "That horse!"

In the evening, sitting on the deck and resting from the day's work, we all would have a cool drink and watch as the little Morgan moved around the campsite, while Reva hovered near him. One night, Clifford came over and began climbing up the stairs of the deck. His hoofs thumped and clattered on the wooden steps.

"Hey!" Mom shouted. "Get off of there!"

"He just wants to come up here and be with us," Dad said.

Reva jumped and snapped. Clifford pinned his ears and trotted off while Dad chuckled.

"Gee, I never knew horses had so much personality," said Mom.

CHAPTER SIX

"The usual rejoinder to someone who says,
'They laughed at Columbus, they laughed at Galileo'
is to say, 'But they also laughed at Bozo the Clown.'"
—*Carl Sagan (1934-1996)*

"Dad, if you decide to ride Clifford while I'm gone, I wish you'd wear my helmet. And if anything spooks him, don't try to stay on. Believe me, he jumps like a rabbit. He will jump right out from underneath you. Don't try to stay with him; you just concentrate on falling good." I leaned against the corral fence and tried not to look worried.

"Hey, now," he said. "Don't you think I know what I'm doing? I rode horses a lot when I was a kid."

I remembered his stories of the big workhorses who had been turned loose and were allowed to roam the entire Island all winter. Dad and Uncle Bob, along with their cousins Red and Norm, used to catch them and ride them bareback through the woods.

"I know, Dad. But I'm telling you, a big horse does not move the way this horse can."

He pooh-poohed me, and I could see a gleam in his eye. He was going to be taking care of Clifford while I was gone, and I couldn't forbid him to ride. I didn't have the heart to, anyway.

I left, and of course one day Dad decided to go riding. He saddled up, climbed aboard and started down the road. They went about a mile, and got to the place where the trees cleared and the ground was raw bedrock. There was thick brush on both sides of the road, and a log lay waiting to ambush Clifford.

He saw it, leaped away from it, and Dad went sailing. Fortunately, he remembered what I had said, and didn't try to hang on. He landed on his seat, but the ground was like concrete there.

Pain blasted through him, and he had to sit still for awhile to absorb the shock. "You bugger!" he shouted at Clifford. "What did you do to me?"

Clifford was nonplussed. His head dropped, lower and lower, until finally his nose nearly touched the ground. He shuffled back over to Dad, meek and apologetic. Dad, despite his sore tailbone, was amused by this obvious display of contrition. He managed to climb on and ride back to camp.

Frank Bailey, Dad's first cousin and youngest son of the original Clifford, was working on the ferry that morning when I headed back to Drummond. He marched up to my window and glared in at me. I rolled the window down and a blast of fresh Lake Huron air blew in.

"What is this I hear about your Dad falling off that horse?" Frank said.

I shook my head. "I know. He told me."

"I want to know why he fell off! Did that horse buck him off? And what's the matter with that stupid horse, anyway?"

"Dad said he spooked at a log by the road."

"A log! What kind of a horse is afraid of a log! You need to put logs in his corral then, so he gets used to looking at them! He can't be jumping around like that with your Dad on his back! That's my Uncle Dudley!"

That was what he called Dad: Uncle Dudley.

"I know." I said. "The colt's only three years old, and has a lot to learn."

"Well, if he's that young, Uncle Dudley shouldn't be riding him! Because if anything happens to my Uncle Dudley…"

I shrugged. "Try to stop him!"

He paused, and I could tell he knew what I meant. Dad was going to do what he wanted to do. I could always stop bringing Clifford up, but that would break Dad's heart.

Dad was sore from his fall, though, and he didn't ride any more that summer.

I did. I had my own adventures, too. One day I rode up into the hard-woods on my grandfather's old farm. I had memories of walking through the mud behind Grandpa's tractor as we made maple syrup back there. I remember thinking, even though I was only four or five years old, how bizarre it was that the trees had faucets sticking out of them, while sap dripped into rusty coffee cans.

The old tub was still there, now filled with dirt and leaves, and I even saw some brown, flattened coffee cans. The maples were adorned with green leaves, now. The forest was silent except for the distant caw of a raven, and the whisper of a soft breeze. Riding along, when we brushed past some saplings, a branch rustled and it startled Clifford. I decided to desensitize him, so the next time we passed under a low branch, I grabbed it and shook it.

He shot right out from underneath me and I sprawled on the cool ground. As he galloped off through the woods, I saw that the saddle was sliding down his side.

Reva stood next to me, confused. "Go get him!" I said, and she took off.

I could hear him crashing away, and imagined that saddle flopping under his belly. I got up and started walking. The worst part about this was the fact that he would run back to camp, where Dad and Bruce were working. I pictured him careening up the road, riderless, and with that saddle askew, and their subsequent panic.

I emerged from the woods and started down the hill, where I found the saddle pad rumpled in the grass. I picked it up and contin-ued walking. I could hear Reva barking, and the roar of a jeep. "Here they come," I thought.

"Where's Nancy?" Bruce's panicked voice shouted.

Around a copse of trees came Reva, with Bruce running right behind her. I smiled and waved. "Hello!"

When we got back to camp, I was surprised to see Clifford not there. They said he had run straight up the road, with that saddle underneath him and the stirrups flapping and urging him on.

Dad and I got in the jeep and followed his tracks. They were widespread, clumps of dirt everywhere.

"Wow, he was really moving," I said.

He had run two miles, and veered off on the road up to what I called Reva's Lake.

We drove up that muddy, bumpy two-track, and Dad said, "There he is."

I squinted. "Where?"

"In those little trees. See him?"

I couldn't. He was camouflaged. Then as we drew closer, I spotted the white blaze on his face. He stood quietly among a clump of young spruce, looking out at us.

We got out and walked over to him. He waited for us. The scarred saddle hung below him, with one stirrup missing. A broken rein dangled from his bridle, and his legs were covered with cuts and scrapes.

"He must have fallen down," I said.

I led him home, while Dad drove on ahead. Clifford walked calmly as the sweat dried on his body. A call to Tess and Alan brought them out with salve, and Alan advised me to call a vet. Clifford needed a tetanus shot and an antibiotic.

He was none the worse for wear though, and up to his old tricks again the very next day when he peeled the seat cover off Dad's tractor.

"Hey!" Dad roared. "You git!"

Reva jumped into the air and snapped at Clifford, and he whirled to gallop up the road. He circled the mill and came pounding back, mane flying. Lewis, Dad's Newfoundland, stood by the camper and barked while Dad laughed.

One day not long afterward, I trailered Clifford over to Hoey's when they invited me to go riding. When I arrived at their farm, nobody was around. The ancient farmhouse stood alone and the horses were out in the field. While I saddled Clifford, I looked across and saw a doe, burnished red in her summer coat. She was watching us from the edge of the woods.

I mounted and let Clifford walk up the road. We went right past the doe. I didn't stop, as I didn't want to scare her. We walked along the gravel road until it curved behind some trees. Then we turned around and headed back. The doe still stood there looking at us, with her dark eyes, wet nose and her large rounded ears.

I hadn't brought Reva, so I thought I'd see just how close I could get. I stopped Clifford, dropped the reins and let him graze. I thought this would surely signal to the doe that we meant no harm. I was close enough to see the soft light reflection in her eyes, the delicate veins in the side of her face. She stood there with her long elegant neck stretched upward, completely motionless except for a tiny flare of her nostrils; a whisper of breath. I wondered if she would come up to us.

When Clifford dropped his head toward the grass, he suddenly spotted the doe. He stared at her for a moment, then whirled and bolted in the other direction.

"Whoa!" I yelled, but it was too late. I was flung backward from the saddle and sailed through the air. I landed on my back and skidded along the gravel road. I could feel the burning hide peeling off my elbow and back.

Realizing he had unseated me, Clifford stopped and turned around.

"It was just a deer, you jughead!"

Tess and Alan arrived then, pulling up in their car. I went riding with them, regardless of my bloody wounds. We rode through miles of woods and fields around their house; past ancient run-down barns and shacks built years ago by Finnish immigrants; through stands of tall and peeling birch trees, into dark tunnels of cedar.

Tess was astride Big John, the massive bay Quarter Horse, and Alan rode bareback on a beautiful gray Arabian gelding named Barney. I envied the way he sat on that horse; the ease with which he skirted every branch and bend in the path. He loved to gallop, and would find any excuse to go flying on ahead of us, bent over the Arab's neck, as much a part of its back as a burr or a tick might be. We would fly along after him through the low-hanging branches, pounding through the leaves and jumping rocks and fallen trees. Tess once looked back at me, gasping for breath, and said, "This is the problem, see. I want to go for a nice trail ride, but Alan thinks he's in the Kentucky Derby!"

Later they invited me out to dinner. So, when we got back to their farm, I put Clifford out to graze in their small pasture by himself, and climbed into the back seat of their car.

"That was a nice ride," Alan said.

"Yes. You know, Drummond isn't really that great a place for riding," Tess said. "You have to be careful to stick to the trails. There are just so many rocks, and crevices in the ground. It can be very dangerous."

I sighed and regarded my reddened arm. "Yeah. The only problem with horses is, they or you are always getting hurt."

In the front seat, I saw Tess's shoulders beginning to shake. She clapped her hand over her mouth but could not smother the uproarious giggling that bubbled forth. Alan looked over at her and smiled quietly. He drove on, and the car passed beneath the ancient trees, with Tess laughing hysterically into her hand.

CHAPTER SEVEN

"Such sweet compulsion doth in music lie."
—*John Milton*

The Fourth of July on Drummond Island was, hands down, the absolute best day of the year. I rode Clifford in the parade, along with Tess and Alan and the Fairchilds, another group of Drummond natives with horses. After the parade, I'd trailer Clifford back to camp and give him some hay. My family would have a cookout, usually roasting whitefish over the fire pit. Mom cooked them with onions and pepper, wrapped up in tinfoil and lying on the grill. My sister Amanda always mixed up a batch of her special tartar sauce. We'd have corn on the cob, baked beans, baked potatoes and salad. Usually some other brothers and sisters showed up, and Aunt Connie and her son James often came too. Old stories and jokes were passed around; new gossip exchanged along with lots of uproarious laughter. Aunt Connie had the female version of Dad's voice: loud and booming. Her laugh was contagious.

Then, as the afternoon wore on, I would saddle up Clifford. He and Reva and I would go off to the little inland lake I called Reva's Lake, or back in the woods somewhere. We would often see deer as they loped across the road, and there were always a myriad of birds: Large, primeval pileated woodpeckers, blue jays, ducks and loons or Canada geese.

The woods were silent except for the breeze, the twitter of sparrows or the call of jays or ravens; a stark contrast to the hubbub I had left behind in town.

The flowers in July were reason enough to visit the Island. The road was lined with clouds of daisies, intermingled with bright yellow black-eyed Susans. Deep orange-red tiger lilies blazed in the shade against the dark ferns, their petals curling outward. Wild iris stood tall, blue jewels in boggy areas. As we approached the lake, growing out of the bedrock were Indian paintbrush, soft bluebells and the delicate red and yellow flowers we called honeysuckle, or wild columbine.

When darkness fell, it was time to head to Aunt Connie's to watch fireworks. We sat in lawn chairs in her front yard, wrapped in blankets. We whooped as the flares jetted up and exploded into shimmering color against the night sky. Considering the size of the community, the fireworks on Drummond were awesome. They didn't hold back. The noise was tremendous; a hollow thump as the flare was ejected, followed by a deafening bang. Brilliant flowers bloomed, one on top of another in the darkness, to fall in glittering bits toward the earth.

I remember one year, when my older brother Ted was home, they seemed to be having trouble with the fireworks. There were long delays between each volley. A few were exploding near the ground, and the flag display toppled.

"Who is doing the fireworks this year?" I asked.

"The Ledys do it," Dad said.

"Which Ledy?"

"Lefty Ledy," Ted replied.

I went into a laughing jag at that, and couldn't stop. Of course there was really no "Lefty Ledy"; not at that point, anyway.

Every year Aunt Connie made strawberry shortcake. Aunt Connie was an avid berry picker and always had a fresh supply of wild strawberries, tiny and plump and crimson, exploding with seeds and sweet juices. She'd take browned, crumbling biscuits from the oven, ladle the berries over them and top each dish off with a generous dollop of real whipped cream. We'd sit in the warmth of her living room, on the floor or by the fireplace or at the piano, and gorge ourselves. Then finally, with calls of "goodnight" and "thanks" all around, we would head for home.

The parade, though, was definitely one of the highlights of this very special day. I was surprised by a revelation one year. It suddenly dawned on me that I could "read" my horse's emotions. Clifford, although then only five years old and pretty green, liked to lead the others, so we took to the front. We were right behind a "Christmas In July" float, all decked in lights and holly. It was transporting a rotund Santa who merrily played the keyboard. The tunes were happy, lively Christmas carols: "Jingle Bell Rock", "Holly Jolly Christmas", and the like.

Clifford was stepping right up, ears perked, and he never turned his head once during that whole parade. He was mesmerized. I swear he was practically bobbing his head in time to the music.

The tones were delightful, and I thought I might be projecting my emotions onto my horse. Could Clifford really have been enjoying the tunes that much? Nah! I was kidding myself. Anthropomorphizing. Not wanting to sound foolish, I didn't mention my thoughts to anyone else.

When the parade ended, I paused to chat with Tess. I said, "Gee, I really enjoyed the parade this year. I think it was our best one yet."

"I know," she said. "I think so too. I think our horses liked the music."

CHAPTER EIGHT

"What do they hunt by the glimmering pools of water,
By the round silver Moon, the pool of Heaven—
In the striped grass, amid the barkless trees—
The stars scattered like the eyes of the beasts above them!"
—W.J. Turner (b. 1889)

"Scritch scritch scritch."

I opened my eyes and looked into the darkness, unsure for a moment of where I was. Then it occurred to me that I was in Mom and Dad's camper. I could hear the whisper of the poplar trees outside. I pulled the sleeping bag more tightly around me, sighed and closed my eyes.

"Scritch scritch scritch."

My eyes popped open. Now I knew why I was awake. The dogs were chewing on something plastic, just outside the window that was right above my bed. I pounded on the window. "Knock it off!"

I heard Reva shift nervously on the deck. Then there was silence.

"Scritch scritch scritch."

Now I knew it wasn't the dogs. I lay still and listened for awhile, trying to determine where it was coming from.

Usually, I enjoyed lying awake at night. I had lived three weeks in the camper, hearing the nocturnal cries of owls, loons and coyotes. After spending the long summer day with Clifford, I would trailer him back to Tess and Alan's, as the sun sank and shadows lengthened. I would feed the dogs in the twilight, then take a book into the camper, and, with the flashlight propped up on a pillow, I would read until the beam grew weak. I was transported to different places with books that Dad had recommended: *"Undaunted Courage"*, the wonderful story of the Lewis and Clark expedition by Stephen E. Ambrose, *"Lonesome Dove"* by Larry McMurtry, or *"Mother Earth, Father Sky"*, by Sue Harrison, a local author from the eastern Upper Peninsula. Dad loved history, and his favorite books were always vivid and captivating.

"Scritch scritch scritch."

My dozing thoughts were interrupted by the noise. I picked up my flashlight and shone it on my watch. It was 4 a.m. I got up and put my slippers on, then took the flashlight and stepped outside. The air was cool, and smelled sharply of spruce. The two dogs greeted me enthusiastically. I shined the light around the deck, but saw nothing unusual. All was silent except for the chirp of distant tree frogs and the excited panting of the dogs.

I went back into the camper, removed my slippers, and climbed back into my sleeping bag.

"Scritch scritch scritch."

I knew I couldn't sleep with this noise.

"Scritch scritch scritch scritch scritch scritch."

I reached for the flashlight again, got up, and crept out the door.

"Scritch scritch. *Scritch scritch scritch.*"

On the deck was a box of empty pop cans, left over from a family cookout. The noise was coming from there, and it was loud. I shined the light over the cans. Inside a clear plastic Coke bottle, I saw something moving. I stepped closer. A deer mouse, trapped inside, bounced up and down, trying to launch himself through the opening at the top.

"Scritch scritch scritch," his claws said, as they slid up and down against the plastic surface.

I picked the bottle up, and it vibrated frantically in my hand as the mouse jumped wildly for the top. I aimed my light at him. I could see his big black eyes, his whiskers, his long pink tail. He had gray fur, a white belly, and little pink feet.

"Come on, Reva," I said. "You have to keep the bears away."

I don't know how far mice will travel to get back home when they are displaced, but one thing was certain: I didn't want mice this close to the camper. So I carried the bottle down the road, turning north to go past the swamp. With me came Reva and Dad's Newfoundland, Lewis (named after Meriwether Lewis, who actually took a Newfoundland on his journey to the West Coast). The dogs leaped joyfully around me as I marched along in my slippers and pink bunny suit, with my flashlight trained on my Mouse in a Bottle.

After I had walked about a third of a mile, I came to a fork in the road and decided that this was far enough for a mouse. I set the bottle down in the grass on its side. The mouse poked his nose out cautiously, then crawled under a leaf and disappeared.

I picked up the Coke bottle, switched off the flashlight, and turned for home. The stars were shining brilliantly above me. The dogs were in ecstasy.

I climbed up the porch steps and shoved the bottle back into the big cardboard box. I went into the camper, pulled off my slippers, and climbed into my sleeping bag. I glanced at my watch. It had taken a half-hour to rescue the mouse.

I sighed and closed my eyes.

"Scritch scritch scritch."

I sat up.

"Scritch scritch scritch scritch scritch."

No! It couldn't be! I turned the flashlight on and looked at my watch. It was fifteen minutes later! I pointed the light through the window, straight into that same Coke bottle. Sure enough, there was a mouse inside, bouncing up and down.

My brain was cloudy with sleep. But I got up, put my slippers on and went outside. I shined my light on him. I could see his big black eyes, his whiskers, his long pink tail. He had gray fur, a white belly, and little pink feet.

I picked up the bottle, laid it on the ground on its side, and went back to bed.

Chapter Nine

"Show me your horse and I will tell you who you are."
—Old English saying

Mom's voice was shaking, sobbing into the phone, "I'm in Traverse City. Dad's got to have a triple bypass. They want him to have the surgery in the morning."

"I'm on my way."

I called Bruce at work and told him where I was going, then flung some things into a bag. It was March 1997, and the house was a mess; moving boxes everywhere. Despite the fact that our home in Dexter had five acres, it was not zoned for horses. I was tired of boarding Clifford, and wanted him to live with us. We had finally found a parcel in the country, but there was no barn, no pasture or trees. There was one lonely house sitting on a hill, surrounded by ten rolling acres of grass and goldenrod and milkweed.

But we had bought the place, and I'd moved Clifford away from Hyatt's farm, to a boarding stable that was closer to our new home. I rushed into the bathroom to get my toothbrush, and it occurred to me that soon, this wouldn't be my bathroom anymore. Change, I realized, was an inevitable part of life, but today an unwelcome one.

Dad had experienced a heart attack several years prior, and had been on a low-fat diet since then. He was trim and fit. He was seventy-one years old that year, still very active and eternally boyish. He had gone to the hospital just for a routine checkup. It must have come as a shock to everyone that he needed this surgery so urgently. As I raced out the door, I thought of the long summers on Drummond, and the man who was so much an integral part of that lifestyle.

"Please God! Let me keep him for awhile!" Fighting back tears, I drove up the road and stopped at the Speedway on the corner. I filled the gas tank and went in to pay. As I stood in line at the counter, I gazed out the window. It was a good four hours to Traverse City, and I didn't know how I was going to stay calm enough to make it.

"You need another three dollars!" a voice snarled, and I turned to see the clerk looking impatient. A couple of other people by now were standing in line behind me. We all were waiting as a little old woman attempted to pay the clerk. She bent over the counter, counting out a pile of pennies and dimes. I did a double take and noticed that it was not snacks or booze she was buying. It was food: A few cans of soup, some tuna, some bread. She counted the change slowly, sliding each coin across the counter from one pile to another.

The clerk shifted, sighed, rolled his eyes. I dug into my wallet, pulled out a ten-dollar-bill and held it out to him. He waved it away. "I'll be with you in a moment!"

"No!" I said. "I am paying for hers!"

"Oh!" He took my money with no apology and went to the register.

The woman turned toward me. Though her hair was wispy and silver, her face was round, and her blue eyes twinkled merrily up at me.

"Bless you!" she said. "You will be repaid one hundredfold for your kindness."

She took her bag of food and walked out, while the clerk counted my change.

As I left the store, I looked for her, but she was nowhere in sight. Time seemed to be turning in a dreamlike state as I got into the Revabus and started it. I felt a sense of complete calm settle over me, and drove to Traverse City with no problem.

A very worried family greeted me. In fact, Dad himself was the only one who wasn't pinched and gray with stress. He came over and stood next to me grinning, with his hands in his pockets, bouncing on his toes.

I made myself smile back at him. "I'll bet you're really looking forward to this."

"Oh, I'm all right. I'll be happy to have it done. Maybe I won't feel so tired all the time."

They wheeled him away the next morning. I don't remember the last thing he said. He'd left the group of us, Mom, my brother Dan and me, standing together like a cluster of sheep.

The hours dragged by. I kept looking at the clock, wondering how long a triple bypass usually takes.

I went down to the cafeteria to find us some snacks, and when I headed toward the elevator, I heard a toddler's voice shrieking, "Daisy! Daisy!"

That was Jacob, Rebecca's son. He called me Daisy because he couldn't say Nancy. I turned to see him running toward me, a grinning and laughing towhead, followed by his anxious-looking mother.

"Ah," I said as I swung him high in the air. "To be this carefree!"

We had been told that Dad would need to be kept very cold during surgery, and that his heart would actually stop beating for awhile. "He'll be dead!" Rebecca said.

"No, they will have machines keep him alive," a nurse told her calmly.

We waited in a room that had a phone, and every hour it would ring. One of the nurses in the O.R. would give us a cheery report of how things were progressing. "He's doing fine! Breathing looks good! Everything looks good!"

With every report, we had to call the rest of the family: Amanda, who was staying with Robin in Gladstone, Ted in Tucson, Jon in Washington state, Raechel in Utah, and reiterate all.

Finally, the surgeon came in. He was a little man, balding, with glasses. He was wearing green scrubs and he grinned and proudly announced that Dad was in good shape. "We had to do a quintuple. It went well."

"I'm curious about something," I said.

"Okay."

"When you stop the heart, how do you get it started again?"

"Well, of course, you use the key."

I stood there and looked at him. I think my mouth was open.

Rebecca suddenly screamed with laughter. "Oh my god, Nancy! It's so funny to finally see someone else do it to *you*!"

The surgeon's lightheartedness cheered everyone. But when we were finally allowed to see Dad in the Intensive Care Unit, the sight of him was a shock to us all. He was pale and so very still and cold.

We didn't stay long. That evening, he was finally coming out of it and he was able to whisper to us a little.

That night, huddled between the sheets in my motel room, I suddenly heard my mother talking. She was speaking to one of my cousins, who was sobbing hysterically. "No, no!"

"It's all right!" I said. "Dad's fine! The surgeon said everything went well."

Mom reached for me, and I felt the scratch of her fingernails on my skin as she tried to grab my arm. "Honey, it isn't alright. Your Dad died about ten minutes ago."

I sat bolt upright in that bed with my heart roaring in my ears. It was dark in the room, and I was alone. It had been a dream; a terrible dream. The telephone was on a table by the opposite wall. I leaped for it and dialed the hospital.

The nurse who answered the phone sounded deceptively calm.

"Could you check on my Dad, please?" I said.

She put me on hold, leaving me waiting in the silence. After several long minutes she came back. "He's fine. He's been restless."

I sighed, relief spilling over me. "So, he can't sleep?"

"He's not sleeping well."

"Ask him if he wants me to come in and sit with him."

I was put on hold again, then she came back a moment later and said, "He's sleeping now!"

I went back to bed and immediately passed out.

When I went in to see him the next morning, he was sitting up eating Jello. He grinned. "Hello, Honey!"

I didn't understand why Jello was the food of choice. Sure, it went down easily, but he was shaky and it was jumping off the spoon.

The Jello plopped into his bowl, and he carefully spooned it up again. "Where's your mom?"

"She went home to Cadillac with Dan."

"Oh. Did you stay with Dan, too?"

"No, I stayed here in a motel. Rebecca had to go back down home, but she'll be back."

"Where's your mom?"

The whole day was like this. He would ask me questions, I would answer them. Then a few minutes later he would ask them again. I was careful to always answer like it was the first time, to never tell him he had asked before.

Robin and Amanda showed up later. Amanda was the youngest, being twenty-six that year, and she had Down's Syndrome. She lived with Mom and Dad, but Robin had gone and picked her up when discovering that Dad was going to stay in the hospital.

Amanda was a stoic character. She had braved many things in her life, including surgery on both knees, and the loss of her hair, which had fallen out due to a dermatological condition. She wore a blonde Princess Di-style wig, and had long white scars on both knees. She was quick to laugh, and had a furious temper, but she rarely cried or expressed emotion when she was worried or hurt or scared.

I was scrutinizing her pretty closely that day, and finally got a chance to take her aside.

"So," I said. "How are you doing?"

"Good."

"Yeah?"

"Yeah." She looked around and then leaned closer to me. "Except Robin pissed me off."

She only used the term "pissed" around me, and only if she was seriously angry about something.

I lowered my voice to a whisper. "Why? What did she do?"

"She called me retarded."

"What? Why in the heck did she do that?"

"She was speeding. The cop pulled her over. She told him I was retarded and I had to see my dad because he was having surgery."

"Did she get a ticket?"

"No."

I paused. "Well, I guess her tactic worked."

"Yeah. It did."

"So, did you say anything to her?"

"Of course!"

"What did you tell her?"

"I called her a freak."

I laughed and held up my hand. "High five!"

She slapped me soundly.

"I guess you handled that."

"Yes, I did."

The days went by and Dad recovered. He was still forgetful, and very weak, but soon he was ready to go home.

Bruce showed up, and he brought my dogs per my request: Reva, Piper the six-pound Papillon, and our newest addition, Scorch the sweet Australian shepherd mix. They jumped and whined and wagged and snorted, giving me wet nose punches and sloppy kisses. I was so happy to see them! We headed back down home that day, to complete the move to the new house.

It was very early spring, with still a layer of snow in lower Michigan, and plenty of snow and ice in the Upper Peninsula. I asked Mom if Dad could come down and stay with me for awhile. He had to do physical therapy to build his strength back up, and I thought it would be easier on them if I drove him to the hospital in Howell every week. They would have to drive the hour to Sault Ste. Marie for his therapy if he stayed up there. Part of his rehab required a daily walk. He could walk outside at my house without fear of slipping and falling, or getting too cold.

He was always reluctant to leave the U.P., so it wasn't an easy prospect to convince him to come.

"Dad, I need help with the new place, planning where the barn will go, and how to set up the new pastures. Will you come down and help me?" I thought that would get him, rather than me offering to play nursemaid. But I did want to play nursemaid. I felt a need to have him close to me, to watch him get better.

He and Mom both agreed that to get outdoors would be good for him, so he came.

He was not himself for the first couple of days. He took long, preoccupied walks around the property. He was quiet; seeming pensive and even depressed. He was still forgetful. He made many comments about how weak he felt, about how he couldn't lift things, couldn't move the way he used to. He would sit silently listening to conversations, instead of leading them with stories (usually lies) and humor, as was his wont in the past. The contrast was remarkable; he was a shadow of his former self. I think for the first time, Dad was face to face with his own mortality. It was like, during surgery, part of him had disappeared and had not returned yet.

He asked to go see Clifford with me one day, so we drove out to the boarding stable. When we pulled into the driveway, I noticed that Clifford was standing way out in the pasture, mowing what bits of grass he could find. He had not seen Dad since the previous fall.

Before I turned the engine off, Dad held a finger to his lips. "Let me call him."

We got out of the truck, walked over to the fence, and stood quietly for a moment. I noticed that the wind was blowing toward us; so Clifford had not smelled us yet. He stood, head down in a grazing trance.

"*Clifford!*" Dad hollered, with his still-mighty voice.

There was no response. Clifford continued to hoover up that grass and didn't even extend the courtesy of lifting his head. I couldn't look at Dad. It was one of the worst possible things which, at that moment, could have happened. I imagined Dad feeling as though he were evaporating.

"Well," Dad said. "Guess he doesn't know me."

"Try again," I suggested; then held my breath and prayed.

So a second time, he bellered, "*Clifford!*"

Suddenly, there was a transformation. *Up* snapped that blazed face, then with a dramatic plunge, the little Morgan jumped forward. Head tossing, mane flying, he kicked up his heels and exploded with a big happy whinny.

"*Grandpa-a-a-a!*" he said, and ta da *dump* ta da *dump* ta da *dump*, his feet sent clods of dirt high in the air as he came rocketing toward us. He crossed the entire acre in about four seconds, then skidded up to the fence, thrust his nose over it and blew warm air right in Dad's face. He stuck his nose on Dad's neck, as if to say, "Hi! Hi! Hi old friend, where have you been? I've missed you!"

Dad's face was wet with tears—I had never seen him so moved. I stood back, letting them commune and resisting the urge to grab and kiss that horse.

That night, over dinner, Dad headed a big discussion about Clifford and all his comical exploits of the past summer on Drummond Island. He happily told Bruce that Clifford had recognized him, and come running, and then jealously chased the other horses away when they came mooching around for treats. He didn't have any trouble remembering that!

I didn't either. I will remember that moment, always, as the time Clifford helped to bring Dad back.

That cherub in the Speedway was wrong. I had been blessed much more than a hundredfold.

CHAPTER TEN

"Be wary of the horse with a sense of humor."
—*Pam Brown (b. 1928)*

The new house stood tall and lonely, like a towering gray ship on the crest of a rolling sea of grass and milkweed. It overlooked a long valley patched with cultivated shades of gray and brown, last year's cornstalks crushed beneath the receding snow. The cold spring wind whistled down the hillside, swirling around the house and the treeless acreage, pushing through dried, aged stems of goldenrod and thistle. The builders' half-hearted attempt at landscaping had manifested itself in the form of several large boulders, hulking in the sparse brown grass of the front yard, not far from the gray outcropping that was the garage.

"This place looks like Stonehenge!" I said. It was obvious that some changes were needed. While Dad recovered from his surgery, we decided to have a shelter built, along with a pasture, that could house Clifford temporarily until a barn could be constructed.

We hired a couple of guys from Dexter who had just begun a brush hogging business. They came out and mowed our entire acreage, the tall dried stalks of goldenrod falling in rows before their machine. Being horse people themselves, they happily volunteered to put up our fence and shelter, and we accepted gratefully.

The fence was up within a day, and I rushed off to trailer Clifford home. He immediately started ripping away at the grass and clover revealed by the receding snow. Sometimes I would peg him out in different areas around the yard, as there was lots of clover closer to the house. With his warm red coat and lively manner, he provided a welcome visual break from the surroundings.

Meanwhile, the two men, Jeff and Bob, began building the three-sided shed. Robin arrived for a visit one day after the frame was completed. She and Dad and I sat in the dining nook, chatting and sipping hot chocolate. From there we had a bird's eye view of the building process, while Clifford ambled around the pasture.

Almost immediately, Clifford began to inspect the construction site with the greatest of interest. He snooped around the area while they worked, sniffing at the tools and stacks of lumber. It wasn't long before he picked up a two-by-four and moved it, dragging it along the ground about twenty feet. Jeff turned around and said, "Hey!"

Clifford dropped the board, did a little skip, and took off. Jeff threw his gloves down and walked over to pick up the board. While he was moving it back, Clifford circled around the structure and picked up one of the gloves. Jeff turned in time to see the horse standing there with the glove in his mouth, waving the fingers delicately in the air.

I was quite sure that by this time, Jeff could hear our hoots of laughter through the windowpane. He gave chase, and Clifford trotted away, head and tail high, long mane blowing in the breeze, carrying his prize. Jeff ran faster, and Clifford finally dropped the glove and stood beside it, waiting.

When Jeff bent over to pick his glove up, Clifford bit him in the butt. I had never seen a guy go so high in the air.

By this time, Robin, Dad and I were in tears from laughing so hard. Jeff led a compliant Clifford through the gate to the back yard where he'd been pegged out earlier, and tied him up. That was where he remained throughout the rest of the construction process. He would graze most of the time, but now and then I would see him watching them wistfully.

CHAPTER ELEVEN

"Anybody can win, unless there happens to be a second entry."
—*Unknown*

I'd been taking dressage lessons on Clifford, and figured it was time to try out my first Morgan show. Clifford was a sturdy five-year-old, having grown and filled out dramatically during the three years I'd owned him.

My friend Sherry had boarded her English Pleasure Morgan, Abby, at the same stable where I had kept Clifford. She had worked for one of Michigan's well-known show barns. She volunteered to help me get Clifford ready, and said he would need to be body clipped. It was early spring and he hadn't shed his wooly winter coat yet.

I didn't know the first thing about body clipping a horse. But Sherry just took over. She had me trailer Clifford over to the barn where Abby was still boarded. She showed up with her own clippers and proceeded to shave him down to the skin. It was a lengthy and painstaking project, even on a horse Clifford's size.

I watched as she clipped him, leaving long pale tracks on his sides and legs.

"How do you like your new place?" she said.

"Oh, it's good. It's really nice having Clifford right at home with us."

"You need to think up a farm name, now."

"We call it Reva Ridge, because it sits up on a hill."

"After Riva Ridge, the racehorse?"

"No, you know, Reva, my dog. And besides, her registered name is Trail Ridge Reva, so it seemed fitting…." My voice trailed off. Sherry was bent over, industriously clipping the inside of Clifford's back legs.

She straightened up, surveying her handiwork, rubbing her forehead with the back of her hand. "Oh yeah. That's a good name. Now you have to pick a signature farm color."

"Oh, well, I've always liked purple. It compliments Clifford's color."

She whirled to face me with an expression of horror. "Oh, not purple! That's a clown color! Nobody will take him seriously!"

"Really!"

She gestured toward the horse with the clippers. "How does he look?"

I stepped back and stared at him. His red hair lay in piles around his feet, and his skin shone through whatever reddish hue of hair that remained on his body.

"He's pink," I said.

"Don't worry, we still have three weeks! It will grow back a little by then. I'll trim his whiskers again when we get there. Just be sure to keep the blanket on him."

Three weeks later, we pulled in at the Mason fairgrounds. Clifford stepped out of the trailer, still wearing his blanket. I had looked for a purple sheet for him, but hadn't been able to find one. But his new purple halter gleamed beautifully in the sun. He looked around with great interest at the crowds of people and horses. The air smelled like manure and wood shavings.

Sherry met me anxiously at the barn. "There you are!"

I did a double take. She had bright red smudges on both cheeks, and was wearing scarlet lipstick. She wore a long yellow gingham dress.

"I'm about ready to go in with Abby," she explained. Most of the women who drove in the harness classes would dress up.

"Oh, we'll come and watch!"

We put Clifford away and then went to watch her class. Abby was a high stepping vision, pulling her cart around the ring at top speed while never breaking her trot. The arena resounded with happy organ music. The shiny dark horses pranced along, harnesses jingling softly as they pulled the lightweight two-wheeled carts. Their drivers were dressed in coats and hats and brightly flowered prints. I half expected each to give a regal wave as they went flying past the stands. Sherry drove with confidence, all the while maintaining a tranquil smile, which I was sure belied her true emotions. The judge stood quietly in the center of the arena with a clipboard, and suddenly each cart lined up, side by side, in the center of the arena. I watched as helpers ran out to grab each horse by the bridle. Sherry's helper had a towel, and was rubbing it over Abby's neck and shoulders as she stood stretched patiently before her cart. The judge wandered formidably among the group. Sherry continued smiling, but her smile was becoming more strained with every minute that passed. Finally, the judge walked over and pointed to Abby. A blue rosette was quietly pinned to her harness, while applause spattered across the stands.

I watched as the other carts left the arena, one by one, while Sherry drove Abby in a victory pass. She whizzed along the rail at a rapid, high-stepping trot, and Sherry now radiated a huge and genuinely happy grin.

As we left the arena, I was thinking how easy that had looked. Surely I could win a blue ribbon too!

Sherry changed quickly after her class and came to help with Clifford. She got out her clippers and shaved off the stubble that was emerging on his chin. She braided his mane and tail. She rubbed him all over with Show Sheen. Then she brushed his feet with black hoof polish. Clifford looked down at his shiny hoofs, and noticed that the corner of the rubber mat was turned up. He reached out and pawed it, pulling the corner up more and more. Sherry gasped and swatted him. "Stop it, Clifford!"

By the time she had finished with the grooming, he still looked pinkish, I thought, but I could almost see my reflection in him. I had donned the traditional Hunt Seat garb; breeches, a dark green coat, some tall boots and a velvet helmet. My shirt was decorated at the throat with a stickpin that had a horseshoe on it. My hair was up in a net. I wore gloves and tiny little horse earrings.

"Are you going to ride him in that snaffle?" Sherry was examining Clifford's bridle. I noticed that her hands were shaking. I could see why she was a little excited. He had become her creation.

"Sure. A snaffle's what he's used to."

"He needs to set his head. I'll lend you my kimberwicke."

Dad and Rebecca arrived while Sherry was adjusting the new bit. It was thick, cold metal and had a chain that ran under his chin.

"Hello, Clifford," Dad said, pulling out a peppermint. I made the introductions.

Clifford was licking and mouthing the strange bit, and attempting to negotiate a peppermint at the same time. His sleek head bobbed and nodded while his naked ears turned back.

I got on and rode out into the parking lot, and then trotted up and down the road a couple of times. Clifford's neck was arched dramatically. "That looks good!" Sherry said.

There were about twelve other Morgans in the class. We got in a line, and then entered the ring one by one. Clifford trotted slowly, but I was happy that he was taking his time. The larger horses blasted past us.

"Road trot!" the announcer said. "Road trot, please!"

This was right up Clifford's alley. The faster he got to go, the happier he was. We were having a grand time in this show. We stretched out and trotted, zipping along the rail. Suddenly, I felt myself bouncing down the side of him. My saddle was slipping. Sherry hadn't tightened the cinch enough; or perhaps she had used too much of that slippery Show Sheen. I could hear Rebecca screaming with laughter.

I righted myself, looked around and saw that the judge wasn't looking. I stuck my tongue out at Rebecca as we passed.

"Walk, please, walk."

Many of the horses were jigging. I knew I only had to give Clifford loose contact, and he would relax and walk. He did. We circled the arena, and I surveyed the others around me. They were dark, leggy Morgans, each of them at least a hand taller than Clifford. He was the only pink one in the class. We were sure to catch the judge's eye.

"Reverse, and trot," the voice over the loudspeaker said.

Using only my legs, I asked Clifford to turn on the forehand, thinking that this would impress the judge. He executed it perfectly, keeping his front legs in place while swiveling his rump around. When we were facing the correct direction, he took about three steps forward, but then started jogging backwards. He was still trotting, with his head set perfectly, only he was moving backward along the rail.

"Give him some leg!" Sherry screamed from the sideline.

I leaned forward and whispered, "Clifford! When he said 'reverse', this wasn't what he meant!"

At first I thought it was another one of his tricks, but then I realized something was wrong.

"Rocky, no! No! No!" a voice behind me shouted, and a large dark horse dashed between the rail and us, knocking Clifford sideways.

"I'm sorry," I called.

"S'okay," she gasped as she and the horse went flying on.

Other horses raced by us, and Clifford continued backing up. Then the ring steward was there, and Clifford stopped to allow himself to be caught. The steward led us to the center of the ring, opened Clifford's mouth and looked inside.

"He has his tongue over the bit," he said softly, reaching in and pulling Clifford's tongue out.

It must have been terribly uncomfortable, having that metal bar jammed under his tongue. No wonder he had tried to get my attention.

I heard Dad's voice rumbling from the stands. "It's that damn bit!"

"Number one-eighteen has asked to be excused from the ring," the voice over the loudspeaker said.

I realized that I was number one-eighteen. But I hadn't asked to be excused! I wanted to keep riding! What about my entry fee? What about all the new clothes I had bought? What about all that preparation, and my blue ribbon?

The judge nodded to me, and Clifford's head dropped as we walked out of the arena.

Sherry met me outside. "Oh, that was too bad. You'll do better next time. But he did look good!"

I took Clifford sadly back to the stable and proceeded to untack him. Dad and Rebecca and Bruce came over and stood watching in empathetic silence. When I released the burnished Morgan into his stall, he lay down immediately and rolled in the shavings. He stood up with flecks of curly pale wood clinging to his body and in his braided mane. He shook himself, stretched his neck and yawned.

Dad walked up, unwrapping a peppermint, and said, "Well. Thank goodness that's over with, eh, Clifford? Now let's go back to Drummond!"

As Clifford crunched the peppermint, it was perhaps only accidental that he seemed to be nodding his head in agreement.

CHAPTER TWELVE

"A friend may well be reckoned the masterpiece of nature."
—Ralph Waldo Emerson (1803—1882)

Clifford developed a habit of standing in the corner of his pasture, gazing wistfully across the field. From there, he could see about a mile across the valley to the distant tree line, which I thought might be pleasant and natural for a horse. But it presented a lonely picture. I started thinking about a companion for him, and as winter drew to a grudging end, I purchased a baby Nubian goat.

The goat was a beautiful neutered male, about the size of a large rabbit, black with long white ears and tan legs. As I pulled back his soft fur, I could see white patches underneath. He was going to be spotted. He had golden eyes and tan hatch marks on his face, and a white spot on his head. He was a goat of many colors. I named him Joseph, the Amazing Technicolor Dream Goat.

Reva immediately adopted him as her own, following him everywhere and watching him closely. I fed Joe with a bottle, and he slept in the garage. I thought when he got a little bigger, he could go live with Clifford. He took daily walks with Dad and me. He would gallop after the dogs, clumsy and lopsided with his ears sticking straight out to the sides.

Dad chuckled. "Doesn't he have a funny little gait?"

I watched the little black goat gamboling up the road after the dogs, with his ears flung out like great white wings. "He looks like the Flying Nun."

It soon became obvious that Joe was not going to be willing to live with Clifford, as had been my plan. He would walk right under the bottom wire, braving the electric snap, to come and lie on the porch with the dogs, stretching his legs luxuriously and grooming himself. When the dogs came in the house, he was very angry not to be allowed in himself. He would leap up on the door, thumping and scraping it with his sharp hooves.

Joe was finally assigned to life in the chain link dog run. He slept in a doghouse at night, and ran loose during the day with his adopted canine family.

This did not solve the problem of Clifford's solitude. It got worse for him, I think, when Dad went back up North. Even though I tried to keep him company, teaching him tricks and playing with him every day, it wasn't like having another equine friend around.

Spring evolved in all its splendor, and Clifford reveled in the new grass. Joe grew tall and lanky. On Memorial Day, the phone rang. I picked it up. "Nancy? This is Sharon Harper."

"Oh, hi Sharon! How are all the Kerry Morgans?"

"They're fine." She got right to the point. "Do you still want to buy Airatude?"

Her timing couldn't have been better, and I wasn't a bit surprised. "Trudy", as they called her, would be three years old by now, and I had known with a settled confidence that she would one day be mine. It was uncharacteristic of me to wait for things with such patience, but who can rush fate?

"Of course I want her! When can I come and get her?"

So it was, after some arguing and pleading with Bruce, that Kerry Airatude graced our lives. If we had ever thought Clifford was little, we thought so no more. He had matured to about fourteen-one hands. Trudy stood at thirteen-two—the same size Clifford had been as a two-year-old. Sharon had many other, taller Morgans; for some reason I was destined to have her little ones.

Clifford was all bravado when we came home with the trailer. His tail was up, and his eyes blazed. I tied him out on his line, and led Trudy quietly down to the pasture. I figured she'd want to have a look around before being inundated with attentions from her curious brother.

Clifford danced on the line, picking each foot up high, moving in slow motion. He seemed suspended in the air, turning his head this way and that. He was tall and proud. He whinnied to her, but Trudy didn't answer. After all, she was recovering from a six-hour trailer ride. She dropped her head to crop the thick grass, and then lay down and rolled.

Finally, I led Clifford through the gate, and he trotted off to see his sister. Trudy pinned her ears, turning her back to him as if to say, "Don't come too close! I might kick you!"

She squealed a couple of times, but that was it. Clifford was smitten with this regal pony, and she became a gracious ruler.

Trudy was dark and lovely. She was quiet, sweet and would stand still while I hugged and kissed her, letting me bury my nose in her mane. She smelled like horse and clover and sweet grass. She never tried to steal anything from my pockets; never thumped her lips or made faces at me. She was kind to everyone; Bruce, Clifford, the dogs, and Joe. She was boss over Clifford, but she would allow him to eat from the same bucket. It was as if they had grown up together. As the place around us grew green and lush, the horses were peaceful together, eating grass in the sun, and all was right with the world.

One day, Bruce and I were busy planting trees, and we let Clifford roam around loose while we worked. I came inside for a drink of water, and looked out the window to see Clifford snooping around where Joe was enjoying the grass. As I watched, Joe went prancing over to Clifford, and Clifford put his head down to sniff noses. Joe responded by putting his own head down, and firmly shoving it up against Clifford's face in a playful goat head-butt. Clifford, to my utter incredulity, pushed back, and the two of them stood locked there, head-to-head, like a pair of sparring Bighorn Sheep. I scrambled for my camera, but the moment passed too quickly.

I described this scene later to my friend Mary as we walked out in the pasture. She said, "No he didn't! You're kidding me!"

Just then Trudy went sailing by, tail in the air, bucking and snorting.

"What's she afraid of?" Mary asked.

"Nothing. She's just playing."

Clifford was right behind her, and we stood in the midst of a churning display of hooves and flying manes, while for about ten minutes the two of them pitched and raced around the field. Finally they ran up by the shed and stood there.

"I think you're making up that goat story," Mary said.

"Clifford!" I hollered. "Come here!"

She turned to watch as Clifford came careening toward us like a bullet. Ta da *dump* ta da *dump* ta da *dump*, so fast, one would assume he would run right by, but then he hit the brakes and did a sliding stop, perfectly arranged so that he was standing a foot in front of me.

"But then again," Mary said. "Your horses aren't like other horses."

CHAPTER THIRTEEN

"It is one of the blessings of old friends
that you can afford to be stupid with them."
—*Ralph Waldo Emerson*

Clifford liked to go, and go as fast as possible, so we had been working very hard on "whoa." I didn't trust my riding abilities, and wanted to teach him to obey my verbals above all else. I wanted Clifford to understand that to me, one "whoa" did not mean, "Slow down." It did not mean, "Keep going until I repeat the command six times." It meant, "*Stop,* right now, no matter what!"

Thanks to my trusty clicker, and the inevitable peppermints, he was getting the message. He got it so well that, when on the longe line, even if cantering, I could call "Whoa", and he would come to a screeching halt. I found that when I was riding him, this abrupt stop had a tendency to nearly put me "through the windshield", but I decided that was all right and we could work on it.

One afternoon, on her way home from school, the little neighbor girl Michelle came to the door. "What's the matter with Clifford? Is he sick?"

"Why?"

"He won't take the clover I'm picking for him."

I ran outside to find him standing by the gate, looking green around the gills. "Yep, he's colicky. Thanks for telling me."

This didn't happen very often; maybe once a year. It was usually easy enough to take care of. If he pooped, he felt better immediately.

I walked him around the yard for awhile, and nothing happened. Since he always pooped in the trailer, I decided to put him in there, to see if it would stimulate the "elimination process". I asked Bruce to look and see if the trailer was stable, since it was parked next to the garage and not hitched to anything. He hollered down the hill a couple of minutes later. "Yeah, it's all ready for you!"

So, I led Clifford up to it and noted that Bruce had even left the door open for us. "How nice!" I thought.

Clifford climbed right in, and I shut the door, hooked him up, and waited. Obviously impatient for the trailer to get moving, Clifford started stomping and jostling around. I didn't mind this, since I thought the motion was probably good for him anyway.

Suddenly, the trailer rolled slowly off its block and began to creep backward.

Quickly, I reached in through the open window and unhooked Clifford.

"*No!*" I shouted. But the trailer didn't listen and continued on its path, down the slope behind our house. I ran around behind it, slammed my body against the back, and *pushed.*

"*Bruce!*" I screamed.

There was no response. I had slowed the trailer a little but Clifford continued to shake it, and it nudged me backward with every move he made.

"*Whoa!*" I hollered.

Bless the little guy's heart, he stopped moving. The trailer paused. I edged over to the door, still leaning on it, and lifted the latch.

Clifford stood quietly while I opened the door. "Okay! Get out."

He backed quickly out of the trailer and trotted off across the yard. The trailer, minus his weight now, stopped rolling. I breathed a huge shaky sigh of relief, and glanced down through the still-open door.

There inside was a pile of poop.

CHAPTER FOURTEEN

"For the animal shall not be measured by man. In a world older and more
complicated than ours they move finished and complete, gifted with
extensions of the senses we have lost or never attained, living by voices we
shall never hear. They are not brethren, they are not underlings;
they are other nations, caught with ourselves in the net of life and time,
fellow prisoners of the splendor and travail of the earth."
—Henry Beston, from "The Outermost House" (1928)

It took the Rookie a long time to learn about bird feeders. I first noticed him one evening in September 1995, while I sat on the deck at camp. I was writing about the day's events, as was my habit. Looking for an evening meal, the birds would come to the feeder, which hung in the gnarled cedar tree beside the deck, a few feet from where I was sitting.

When I looked up, the Rookie was hovering near the translucent plastic, picking at the sunflower seeds which were mixed with the less desirable millet. His beak tapped the plastic with a futile clicking noise as he tried to get at the black seeds, so close but so inaccessible. The other chickadees flew straight to the perches, taking the millet and whatever else was available through the feeder's stingy little holes.

Not the Rookie! He slammed himself against the sides of the feeder, wings flickering noisily. He wanted those sunflower seeds, and he was aggressive! Angrily he chased the other birds away, frantically defending the feeder even though he couldn't reach the seeds himself.

The next day, he was back, sitting grudgingly on the perches and eating the millet. Now and then I saw him wistfully pecking at the plastic where a sunflower seed tantalized him.

I got out a bag of bird food and poured a dozen black sunflower seeds in my hand. The Rookie eyed me suspiciously as I held them out, but he cocked his head and looked them over. Flinging himself off the feeder, he swooped down, dashed through the air, and then up again. He dive-bombed my hand a few more times, testing me. I didn't move.

Finally, he landed on my fingers, looked at the seeds and then up at me. His claws were like little needles. I was surprised by the heft of him. He was a ferocious, solid little guy. He sat unmoving for a moment, his eyes glittering in the black cap, his buff-colored breast feathers unruffled. Finally, he snatched a seed and took off.

I waited, unmoving. He came back. Pretty soon he was picking up two seeds at a time and flying off with them. He made seven or eight return trips, until they were gone.

The next morning, as I sat writing in my bedraggled notebook, the Rookie tried out a begging technique. He sat on a branch looking at me, every now and then saying, "Chip. Chip."

I never thought it would be possible to tell chickadees apart from one another. The Rookie stood out mainly because of his behavior. He was the most bossy and aggressive among them. He was certainly the boldest. While the others fluttered and squabbled at the feeder, he kept an eye on me. Occasionally he would land on the toe of my shoe, and then take off again. I knew he was a wild bird, but I sometimes liked to think that he had become sort of attached to me, in a way. I supposed that was just my own human ego's sentiment. After all, what use would a wild bird have for a person? It was all about survival, I guessed.

I got into the habit then of keeping a handful of seeds ready, and holding them out to him when he appeared. He would invariably fly down, sit on my hand, take two seeds and then fly away.

I found myself having a blooming interest in ornithology that year, as I realized I could identify many birds by the sounds they made. During my long rides with Clifford and the dogs, back to Reva's Lake, I could hear the croak of a heron, and look to see its huge pterodactyl wings as it flapped away from a dead tree branch. Nearly every day, I saw a king-fisher hunting over the lake, flipping and shooting down into the water, coming back out with a tiny fish in its oversized bill. The kingfisher had a distinctive chatter that I learned to recognize.

My wildlife art background had given me an education in duck vari-eties. I saw many, many of them on our trail rides; mallards and mer-gansers, buffleheads and canvasbacks. Loons were common and very distinctive; both in their call and their appearance. There was no mis-taking that long, low mysterious whistling howl, or the shrill giddy laughter that came peeling in to shore through low-lying clouds of fog.

Bald eagles were becoming more and more prevalent in the Upper Peninsula. Ospreys frequented the bays and islands around Drummond. And hawks were everywhere—red-tailed and sharp-shinned and broad-winged. To my delight, I saw a number of colorful little kestrels—or spar-row hawks—too.

Owls were less easy to spot. At night they could be heard. One night I did see a great gray owl doing amazing aerobatics around a street light, twisting and diving to catch the hoards of moths that fluttered there.

There were many times during my rides when the explosive wings of a partridge, as it leaped out of thick cover and flew off, had startled Clifford and nearly unseated me.

One day while riding in the woods, I heard the very loud and distinc-tive sound of what Dad called a "shypoke", or "pile driver". He had described the noise as, "ker-plunk, ker-plunk, ker-plunk" and that's exactly what it sounded like. I looked up pile driver in the bird book, and found that he had been referring to the American Bittern.

In 1996, when Clifford was five years old, Dad got busy building a garage at camp. It included a stall for Clifford, which served as a run-in. The Rookie came back that year, followed by a baby that twittered and buzzed and blurred its wings at him. I saw him feeding it once. It was undoubtedly the Rookie, because he chipped at me, and when I answered, he came and took two seeds. Again, my ego piped up and said that perhaps he had come to show me his child. "That's a very handsome baby, Rook," I told him.

This became the Year of the Chickadee, because the dam of evasiveness broke, and there were chickadees everywhere. They followed Dad and me around the campsite, having quickly learned that our pockets were always full of seeds. While I was tacking Clifford up, they would land on the saddle. They would sit on our shoulders and heads. They would ride with Dad on his tractor. One of them flew in his open truck window when he pulled into the campsite one morning. They would perch on the fence while I cleaned the corral, and follow me down the road when I went to dump the manure. The trees were laden with them. They shone in the sun like little silver ornaments, flying here and there to position themselves so they could watch us. They had a seemingly insatiable appetite for sunflower seeds. It got so that I could point to a bird in any tree, and it would come shooting down, land on my hand, take a seed and fly away again.

"Look at this!" I said to Dad one day, as they hovered over and around me. "I feel just like Snow White!"

The chickadees were accompanied that year by two red-breasted nuthatches. Dad called them "upside-down birds", because of their habit of walking down a tree, facing the ground. These birds were more aggressive than the Rookie had ever been. The darkest one, whom we called Bingo, would come zooming and beeping to my hand, grab three or four seeds in his long beak, and go zipping off again. If seeds were not produced, he became very demanding. He would fly right in our faces, or land in our hair. He buzzed around Dad as he worked on the barn roof. He scared visitors. We couldn't really think of him as a pest, because he was so pretty. His feathers were dark gray, and he had a black stripe over his eye, and his breast was a vivid russet color. He was very friendly, too; he just knew what he wanted. He was sort of like the kid in the back of the classroom who is disruptive, but well meaning, and everyone can't help liking him.

The birds became more frantic as winter approached, grabbing as many seeds as they could, and racing off to store them in the cracks and nooks which only birds can find. They would come back immediately for more.

The following spring there were fewer birds, and Dad said he thought they were nesting. I looked for the Rookie all that year, but did not see him. Other regulars came; the shy one, smaller than the others who, once she got the nerve to land on your hand, would sometimes take a seed, sometimes not; and Spotty, who had a distinctive white spot on his head and always preferred to take his seeds from the ground.

I heard nuthatches beeping in the woods, but Bingo did not return, nor did his friend. I figured wild birds, especially the little ones, probably had a life span of only a couple of years. I especially missed the Rookie, who after all had been first among them. I felt a little sad. I consoled myself with thinking that perhaps one of the birds we fed this year was his offspring.

Then in 1998, I was standing on the deck one cool September morning, and I heard a familiar call. "Chip. Chip." I reached into my pocket, conditioned after all this time to feed chickadees who spoke to me. I glanced over, and sitting on the cedar branch was a bird who looked at me with first one eye, and then the other.

"Well," I said. "Come on."

I opened my hand, revealing the smooth black seeds. He flew to me in an instant, just as another bird tried to light. He spread his wings ferociously, parting his beak in an avian threat. The other bird left in a hurry. He studied my cache, then carefully selected a seed. He turned it sideways in his mouth and reached for another.

I gasped. "Rookie! Is that you?"

He cocked his head, sitting with his mouth full, his nails digging confidently into my finger. Then he flew off.

CHAPTER FIFTEEN

"Treat the earth well.
It was not given to you by your parents,
it was loaned to you by your children."
—Ancient Native American Proverb

"Hey Nancy, it's Rhonda. I'm headed out to Novi to the Horse Expo. Wanna go?"

Those words were enough of an invitation for me. Each November, the big Novi Horse Expo provided a smorgasbord of horse vendors—tack, equipment, feed, art, and they even had stalls and trailers and carriages. There were demonstrations of all types; barrel racing, dressage, training, and a parade of breeds. The horses were stalled in row upon row, and there was always a fascinating variety of equines to look at. My friend Rhonda had one old Morgan mare, and a couple of Tennessee Walkers, so we always paid special attention to those breeds.

Crowds of horse lovers showed up. There was a variety of spectators: cowboys in their boots and hats, teenage girls in athletic jackets touting various stables, women in heavy fleece coats with horse designs embroidered on them.

We looked at tack and riding apparel, and stopped and browsed the horse books that were available. Many were old and out of print. We laughed and squealed over books like "Misty of Chincoteague" and "King of the Wind", and the "Black Stallion" series. We searched eagerly for a copy of "Justin Morgan Had a Horse", but alas, there were none to be found.

We wandered past the booths provided for various Michigan trail riding and breed groups, stopping of course to pore over breed brochures at the Michigan Justin Morgan Horse Association booth.

As we walked past the table featuring the Michigan Carriage Drivers group, I stopped in my tracks. Not immediately noticing my abrupt halt, Rhonda kept walking for a few steps before she turned around.

On the table was a picture of a horse pulling a Meadowbrook cart through a creek. But it was not the horse that caught my eye. It was the creek, and the sparkling blue bay behind it, shining in familiarity. I suddenly felt an ache of terrible homesickness; and a sort of jealous invaded feeling. The photo was of the place I called Clifford's Bay, and seeing it in this venue was rather like having my backyard put on display.

Clifford's Bay was special to me in many ways, a historical and private place. It was the spot where my great-grandfather, George Warren Bailey, had anchored his boat when he and his wife Cornelia had first arrived to settle on the Island, back in the 1800s.

I had taken many rides there, with Clifford and Trudy and Reva and Scorch. The last time we had crossed that creek, I'd noticed a group of perch suspended in it. As Clifford waded through, the mass of them darted around in confusion. They swarmed ahead of us, and I slowed Clifford a little. I wondered just how far up the bank his four splashing legs could chase them.

They gradually split up, of course, and zipped past us, except for one who in its panic raced higher and higher into the shallows. It finally flung itself up into the mud, where it lay on its side, staring helplessly, gasping and flopping.

"Look at that, Clifford!" I said. "You can bring home the bacon!"

I shooed the dogs away from the fish, got down and put him back in the water. He vigorously darted off, a shadow in the creek.

Standing there in the crowd, it took only a moment for all these thoughts to pass through my head, but Rhonda must have noticed a change in my expression. "What's the matter, Nanc?"

I indicated the photograph. "That was taken on Drummond Island."

The woman sitting behind the table smiled brightly. "That's right! How did you know?"

"That's my home."

"Oh, you're so lucky!" Her tone rang with a wistful sincerity.

Suddenly, I felt better. The carriage horses, after all, had come and gone. I remembered the day they rode past camp; carts and horses and happy people. Clifford and Trudy had trotted and called to them as they went down the road.

I had followed their tracks later, and as I recalled, the group hadn't left trash anywhere. I realized these were the types of guests we wanted on the Island. They had left only tracks, and apparently had taken only pictures.

I smiled at her. "Yes, I am. Very lucky. Come back any time."

CHAPTER SIXTEEN

"To watch us dance is to hear our hearts speak."
—*Hopi saying*

The Morgans were beside themselves that day. It was December 1997 and we'd had a blizzard the night before, with grainy snow falling horizontally. It accumulated to about six inches, with drifts. It was clean and bright and had settled softly on the trees. I looked out the kitchen window to see Clifford do little hop, arching his neck and shaking his head around. Trudy liked to stand on her hind legs, and she pirouetted around in circles with her front feet pawing the air.

Clifford dashed up to her, and then away again, and off they went, tails high, manes blowing, flinging clods of the white stuff high in the air with their flying hooves.

I watch them, laughing at their antics. Then to my amazement, Clifford stopped, turned to face Trudy, curled up one front leg, and bowed! He bowed down low, tucking his head and pressing his face flat into the snow. I thought my eyes were playing tricks on me, but then he did it again! He stood up, pawing at the snow a little, and then bowed like a gentleman.

Clifford had been taught to bow, but I had never seen him do it on his own. Now I realized that he was doing it exactly as I taught him: Curl up the left front, extend the right, arch the neck, and then down. Each time he bowed, he did it like this, with precision. His bow had never been so graceful or elegant.

Watching their maneuvers in the snow reminded me of the goal of a dressage rider; to make the horse look as natural as possible. I had seen the Lipizzaner stallions from the Spanish Riding School perform once years before. It was beautiful and precise, art imitating life. And now Clifford and Trudy were life, imitating art.

CHAPTER SEVENTEEN

"There is no secret so close as that between a rider and his horse."
—*Unknown*

Bruce had driven the hour to work one icy winter morning, in his little Dodge Neon, full well knowing that a blizzard was predicted.

Sure enough, the snow came down. As the hours passed, the driveway at Reva Ridge, which is hilly and about a third of a mile long, was overblown with three and four foot drifts. I received a forlorn call from Bruce, who was still at work. "I'm about to leave. How does our driveway look?"

"I'll see you sometime next week," I replied.

He told me sadly that he didn't mind walking home, but the biggest problem was he hadn't brought his boots. He would have to make the trek through the snow in his dock siders.

We didn't own a four-wheel drive that year. I waited for awhile, then went out to the barn and saddled up Clifford and Trudy. It was pitch black by that time, around 7:00 p.m. The snow was still falling and blowing, glistening under the porch lights. The horses blew warm breath on me softly, eagerly anticipating this sudden adventure.

I got on Clifford and ponied Trudy up the hill behind the house. Our motion sensor came on, brilliantly flooding my retinas and blazing off the white snow. I couldn't see a thing. Clifford stopped.

"It's okay, go on," I told him. He remained rooted to the spot. "Go on!" I insisted, and he moved forward and plunged straight down into the hole by our driveway. I realized what was happening and let go of the lead rope. Trudy, of course, was far too smart to follow when she didn't have to.

We were in the bottom of the gulch, with Clifford in snow up to his belly. I looked up at the house as my eyes became readjusted to the dark. Obviously, we hadn't been where I thought we had. He had tried to tell me. Now what? He stood quietly waiting for directions, as I looked around. There was cold, wet, waist-deep snow on each side of me. Well, I wasn't about to get off.

I grabbed the saddle horn. "Okay, let's go!"

He gathered himself and began leaping through the drifts while I hung on for dear life. When finally he climbed up the other side, Trudy stood waiting for us happily. We resumed our trek.

The driveway had disappeared and was now a huge snow field. We plowed through it all the way up to the mailbox, and the Neon's headlights flashed over us.

"Wow!" Bruce shouted, as he got out of the car. "This is just like the old days!"

He went on to gush about how glad he was not to get his feet wet, and how cool it was that I had thought of this. And that I was so smart! Brilliant, even!

I just smiled, and said nothing. But I thought I heard Clifford give a little snort.

CHAPTER EIGHTEEN

"Who knows if the spirit of man rises upward
and if the spirit of the animal goes down into the earth?"
—*Ecclesiastes 3:21*

Joe the Goat was sick. He was lying in the stall one morning, and didn't get up when I opened the door. I remembered that I had given him popcorn the night before. I called the vet, and she came out. She did tell me popcorn was not a good thing for goats to have.

We treated him for bloat. I rubbed his wide, warm tummy, and put him on a leash and made him walk around with me. Dr. Cawley told me to "drench" him with mineral oil. I put it in a big syringe and shot it down his throat. She had said to be careful not to get it into his lungs, as goats could get pneumonia very easily. It was a messy business, and Joe didn't like it. It ran out the sides of his mouth and it was impossible to tell how much he was getting.

He wandered around on the early spring grass, not eating much. It was sad to see him this way; he was normally so lively. His long ears hung down morosely; no longer did they stick out or wiggle or point in different directions.

As the week passed, he remained off, but then one day he seemed to feel a bit better, finally nibbling at the grass, and I even gave him some grain.

The next morning, I came out to the barn to find him stretched out in his stall, cold and stiff, with his eyes staring lifelessly ahead.

I ran back to the house. It was the weekend, and Bruce was upstairs getting dressed.

"Joe's dead!" I wailed.

He went out to the barn and I watched from the bedroom window, sobbing, while he dug a hole in a sunny spot near the back of the property.

I was plagued by guilt. I had fed Joe popcorn, and it had killed him. How could I have been so stupid? Why hadn't I checked to see what would be okay to feed him, and what not?

Later that day, I noticed that about six inches of Clifford's mane had been neatly snipped off. Joe had learned to open the Dutch door from inside his stall. I remembered how he would stand with his front feet over the bottom half, bleating and communing with the horses. He must have chewed on Clifford's mane, while Clifford stood there and enjoyed the attention.

It occurred to me then that if Joe had swallowed that hair, it could have blocked his intestines. I wondered how long this had been going on. How could I not have noticed?

I never did feel I had done right by Joe. He should have had his own pasture, and a goat friend to keep him company. He shouldn't have had to live in a dog pen, and been stalled at night. I was really tormented by his death; bothered by the many things I had done wrong. I was still thinking the popcorn may have had a role in killing him. And if the mane chewing had killed him, why hadn't I paid more attention, and put a stop to it?

Then a couple of nights later, I had a dream. I was standing in the backyard, surrounded by brilliant emerald grass and bright yellow dandelions. Joe came skipping out of the barn toward me. He was shimmering ebony and white. His ears shone. His edges were blurred, as if he was in soft focus. He came over and nuzzled my leg, but somehow I knew not to touch him. He lay down next to me and chewed his cud, the ultimate sign of Goat Trust and Contentment. Then, after a few moments, he got up, and a tree-lined road opened up before him. He cantered off down the road, with that funny gait, and his ears out. A quiet message came to me saying, "It wasn't your fault."

It was by far the most beautiful and colorful dream I'd ever had. When I woke up, I felt the burden had been removed. And how fitting that Joe should leave my life in a vivid dream.

He was truly, after all, the Technicolor Dream Goat.

CHAPTER NINETEEN

"The secret of eternal youth is arrested development."
—Alice Roosevelt Longworth (1884—1980)

"Aunt Nancy, can I please please pleeeeease ride your horse?" Allison looked up at me through her glasses. "I brought my helmet."

Clifford had just been turned loose in the yard to mow the good grass, and he had been squealing and bucking before settling down to graze. I thought he probably wouldn't appreciate the interruption. But Allison didn't own a horse, and she lived seven hours from me, up in Gladstone. She didn't get a whole lot of opportunity to ride.

"Sure, you can ride him. Hey, Cliffy!"

Up popped his blazed face, and his ears perked forward with interest as he ambled over to us. I led him into the barn and tacked him up. Despite the fact that he had been playing earlier, I knew I had nothing to worry about. He would take good care of the little girl. I didn't bother to warm him up, though part of me wondered if he'd find a way to make a statement.

Allison followed me around the barn. She was twelve, and a nice enough kid, I thought, but she had a serious case of diarrhea of the mouth. She prattled on, nonstop, whether you were listening or not. I handed her a brush, and she began brushing Clifford's shoulder. "Hey, Aunt Nancy, what kind of horse is Clifford?"

"He's a Morgan horse."

"Does he have papers? A family tree, and all that?"

"Sure."

"Does he have some kind of fancy name? Like 'Sir Lord Clifford of Wind Wood' or something?"

I plopped the saddle on Clifford and glanced down at her, briefly wondering where she had come up with that one. "His name is Kerry B Proud."

"How do you get Clifford out of *that*?"

"Well, I had to call him something for short. Anyway, you had a great, great Uncle Clifford, your grandpa Bailey's dad's brother, who lived up on Drummond Island. That's who he's named after."

"Oh." She brushed for a moment, then said, "I think his fancy name should be, 'Clifford of Drummond Island.'"

I smiled. "Okay, come on."

I led Clifford out of the barn and asked him to stand. Allison climbed aboard, and I led Clifford to a flat spot in the yard and began giving her an impromptu riding lesson. She didn't know how to steer him, letting the reins just hang, and Clifford kept walking over to stand with his nose in my face.

"Shorten your reins!" I would say. She finally started doing better, but then began just going aimlessly in circles. Finally, I decided to use some orange cones to help guide Allison, to give her a target to steer toward. I ran off to the barn and came back with a couple of them.

"Now, you just wait right there," I said. Clifford stood patiently with the little girl astride. I turned and began placing the cones on the ground, about fifteen feet apart.

Behind me, I heard a squeal. *"Aunt Nancy!"*

I turned around, and there stood Clifford, with the helplessly giggling Allison still aboard. He was holding one of the cones in his teeth, waving it at me furiously while the reins flapped and his eyes rolled.

Chapter Twenty

"Life is a succession of lessons which must be lived to be understood."
—Helen Keller

In June the heat settled into lower Michigan before I could make my escape to Drummond. I decided to start leaving the Morgans out on grass at night, and letting them cool off in the barn during the hottest part of the day. That would give them a little break from the flies, too. It was so nice for them to stand in their stalls, with a breeze coming through the open Dutch doors, where they could snooze away the afternoon.

That evening I had let Clifford loose in the yard while I put Trudy in the pasture. Clifford had been given a lot of controlled freedom in his life and he had, as we say in dog training, "A reliable recall." Besides, he adored Trudy and always followed her. But that night he wouldn't come. He took off running, as if to say, "You can't catch me!"

Of course I was chasing him all over the property like a dingbat. He took a few bites of grass here and there, which only rewarded his endeavor, flicked his tail and took off again.

Finally it dawned on me that I needed to use my cerebral cortex, because I was never going to run Clifford down. So, I got Trudy and put her back in the barn. Trudy the Good came immediately, allowed me to slip her halter back on, and was led peacefully into her stall, and given a little grain. Clifford the Bad continued alternating grazing/galloping. Finally he noticed that he no longer had an audience, and started looking for his sister. Lo and behold, she was in the barn. He walked in, only to have me slide the door shut behind him.

He knew he was in big trouble! He rolled his eyes at me while I snapped the longe on him, and out the door we went. He then spent the next twenty minutes trotting on the longe, working up a sweat. (Moral: Unpleasant things happen when you do not comply.)

I put him in crossties then, with a nice breeze blowing through the aisle so he could cool off. When he cooled down, he went back in his stall. Trudy the Good went outside to eat the green pasture grass.

Clifford was angry at being left behind. He sulked in the corner. I opened the stall door, offering his halter so he could come and put his head in. He could see Trudy the Good by hanging his head out the Dutch door, so stood with his back to me and stared at her longingly. I left him there. He had hay in his stall to munch, but he really wanted me to open the Dutch door so he could go be with his sister. I gave him a couple more chances to come to the halter that night, but he always turned away, so…

Oh well!

Trudy was unruffled by his predicament. She would wander up to the water tank for a drink, and say hello to him briefly. But then she'd go out on the grass again, leaving him leaning over the Dutch door and snapping his tail in annoyance.

Besides his halter maneuver, Clifford had learned a number of tricks with the help of the clicker. He could bow, nod his head "yes", shake his head "no", "count" with one front foot, "walk fancy", picking each front foot up high and arching his neck, and retrieve. The retrieving was perhaps the most glamorous of his tricks. I had a small plastic cone that I would throw, and he would take off at a gallop, pick it up, trot back with it and put it in my hand. I was constantly brainstorming trying to come up with new stuff to teach him.

I realized that, with my clicker training sessions, I had always been wearing a fanny pack, which held a variety of treats: carrots, cut up apples, peppermints. The sound of the click told him that one of these delicacies was on the way. That day, when I had tried to catch him, I was sans the fanny pack. When I approached him in the stall, no fanny pack. I decided I wanted him to behave himself without the bribery of a visual cue.

He stayed alone in the stall all night. The next morning, I went to the barn, and opened his stall door, and held out the halter. He turned away. So, I slid the door shut, walked away, and went into the feed room. I got a can of grain, shook it enticingly, ignored Clifford the Bad and took the grain outside to Trudy the Good.

An hour later, I came out to the stall to try again. This time, Clifford the Bad eyed me suspiciously, but did not turn away. "Come here!" I coaxed, smiling and shaking the halter invitingly.

I could almost see him working it out. Finally, he stepped grudgingly over, and put his head in the halter.

Click!

I could literally see the surprise in his eyes when he heard that familiar, rewarding sound, and out of my *pocket*—no fanny pack anywhere—came a treat!

Wow! This was great! He stuck his head into the halter again, and got a click and a scoop of grain. The next time he stuck his head in, he was taken out of the stall, groomed, and taken outside to finally be with Trudy, his Good Sister.

Clifford was seven years old by that time, and still challenging my brain cells regularly. I guess he didn't want me to get too relaxed.

CHAPTER TWENTY-ONE

"God is a comedian, playing to an audience too afraid to laugh."
—Voltaire

Though adamantly not a horse person, Bruce had graciously agreed to accompany me to the Michigan Justin Morgan Horse Association's spring trail ride. Anne Wyland, of Ancan Morgan farm in Davison, Michigan was hosting the ride.

Bruce checked the tires on the trailer, helped me load the gear, and drove. We were supposed to be there at noon; but being late was a habit for us—and we were further delayed by road construction. We pulled the trailer in the Ancan farm's driveway about four minutes after Anne and the other riders had left. Apparently the gentle rain wasn't going to hinder their plans.

I had a backpack with some cold packs and bottles of Coke. We quickly unloaded the Morgans, saddled up, Bruce donned the backpack and we took off.

I led on Trudy, so "Zoom-Zoom" Clifford wouldn't take off with the tenderfoot. Clifford liked to lead, but always at his own pace: Accelerated.

Access to the trail required us to ride along a busy highway. Trucks and cars came roaring past us as we picked our way along through the drizzle. Suddenly, I heard a loud "*Smack!*" followed by an expletive. I turned around to see a can of Diet Mountain Dew lying erupted in the road with foam spewing violently out of it. Bruce held the strap of the backpack. "It broke," he said.

We had no choice but to go on, leaving the pop can in the road. We had no way to clean up the mess and the traffic was too busy to risk stopping. At my urging, he tied the backpack around Clifford's saddle horn, and we turned down the side street toward the trail.

"*Pop!*" I heard, followed by more cursing. I looked around and, sure enough, in the road lay the backpack. One of the Coke bottles sprayed a tan fountain of froth across the pavement.

"Well, that's two down, one to go!" I said cheerfully. "Sure glad it's one of *my Cokes* that's left!"

"Do you care about that pack?" he said. "Why don't we just leave it here?"

It had been a gift from my parents. "Well, we shouldn't just leave it. I'll get it."

But he dismounted and, grumbling, picked up the frayed pack and cleaned up the mess while Clifford looked around with interest. He climbed back on and we departed again. "Well, let's see if we can get another quarter mile!" he snarled.

We made it to the woods, where the trail veered sharply, and we followed the tracks left by the group of Morgans. The air was sweet with blossoms stirred by the rain.

"We'll have to hustle if we want to catch them," I said.

We took off at a trot, Clifford the eager leader and Trudy closely following over the rough ground. Curses and groans floated back to me as Bruce jerked and bounced in the saddle. The trail curved and twisted, and we rode under low hanging branches that whipped and scratched us.

"Isn't it pretty back here?" I enthused.

I continued to admire the scenery while we hurried through the brush. Finally, we caught up with the group. There were perhaps ten other horses, most of them beautiful, and unmistakably Morgans. I met Anne and several other people, and we chatted happily. "That's a beautiful mare!" someone said, indicating Trudy.

"Why, thank you!" I reached down and scratched her neck. I heard several more compliments on Trudy's beauty and conformation, and the pretty way she moved. I reflected that even Raechel had liked her, and had made no comments on her diminutive size.

Every now and then someone pointed a camera at us, and every time I looked at Bruce, he was scowling, soaked tendrils of hair dripping down on his forehead.

"This is the longest afternoon of my life!" he muttered.

I just laughed. "I bet you will never go riding again!"

I didn't feel too sympathetic. I was having too much fun.

Finally, the time came to go back. Anne had a big spread of food waiting, under a canopy out of the rain. As we unsaddled the horses, I said gleefully to Bruce, "Isn't it funny? All that trouble with the backpack, and we never even took a break and drank that last Coke! Why, we could have just left that backpack right here in the truck!"

I took the Coke out of the pack, and walked toward the hot dogs that were roasting on the grill. As I unscrewed the top, I suddenly was sprayed, head to toe, with sticky foam, as the bottle said, "Pssssssssssssst!"

I looked back to see Bruce doubled over, laughing.

CHAPTER TWENTY-TWO

"A man of courage is also full of faith."
—*Marcus Tullius Cicero, Roman Philosopher*

"If you can't find anyone else to ride Clifford in the parade, I'll go," Dad said.

I laughed. "That sounds like a pretty reluctant offer!"

It would be Trudy's second Fourth of July parade. The first time, she had been going under saddle for exactly eight weeks, but I didn't hesitate to take her. She had done well, as I had known she would. Bruce had ridden Clifford that year. This year he was immersed in a project and couldn't come North. I wanted to ride Trudy, now four years old, to give her the experience. It did seem a shame, though, to leave Clifford behind, especially when he enjoyed it so.

I was trying to get Dad to go with me. To honor him, though, I asked Rebecca if she'd like to go.

"Are you kidding?" she said. "With my back problems?"

"Looks like it's up to you, Dad."

I could tell he didn't want to. He was having some residual cautious feelings since his open-heart surgery two years prior. Worse, the last time he had ridden Clifford was the time he had fallen off.

"You don't have to," I added.

"No, it's all right. I'll do it. Clifford and I understand each other."

We pulled into the driveway down by the museum, where the parade was starting. Floats were gathering and a group of horses stood around while their riders talked and laughed amongst themselves. Tess and Alan waved to us, and Dad paused to talk to them.

While he was thus engaged, I unloaded Clifford and grabbed his halter, pulling his head close.

"You take care of him!" I whispered.

I tossed the western saddle on him. Clifford was neck reining quite well now. I had spent the past three weeks using the clicker to teach him, because it was the only way Dad knew how to ride.

Trudy was going English, and although she had only been here once before, with all these floats and balloons and flags and people, she didn't get excited or snort. She just stood tied to the trailer, looking around with an expression of equine wonder, her eyes dark chocolate, large and liquid.

The antique cars on the road near us began to edge forward.

"It's starting!" I said.

Dad came over and I held the off stirrup while he climbed aboard. Getting on was difficult for him, because he had a bad knee. Clifford stood perfectly still while he mounted. Tess and Alan had moved off with their horses, and Clifford turned, impatient to go.

Dad just let him go, ambling off down toward the road.

"Jeesh!" I said. I was in a panic. How was I going to keep an eye on him this way? I flung myself on Trudy and trotted after him.

Clifford stepped out and walked right to the front of the group of horses, as was his habit. Trudy sidepassed by some balloons, eyeing them with suspicion. I kept watching Clifford, however, and urged her up close to him. My black dog Scorch, who always accompanied us, pranced along happily, pausing to greet people in the crowd.

"Hello, Forrey!" Dad hollered, raising his hand to wave. "Hello, Thelia!"

Clifford walked calmly, straight and even, with his ears forward. He flinched at nothing. The car ahead of us would stop, and it was an old car so it would make a horrid rumble when they revved it up. Clifford just stood and waited until it moved on again. The other horses in the group jittered and danced now and then. Trudy saw things occasionally that caused her to take a funny step. Clifford just walked.

I looked over at Dad. He was grinning hugely, sitting up straight on the little horse. He was waving like a king. His relatives everywhere called to him. Shouts of "Blaine!" "There's Blaine!" echoed in the summer air.

We came down the shady street approaching the farmhouse where my grandfather had been born nearly a hundred years prior. Two dark and ancient pine trees, with trunks as big as silos, towered over the road.

Dad turned to me. "I've got to go say hi to Bernice."

He nudged Clifford and rode across the lawn, up to the rambling porch where his cousin Bernice Holmes sat. She was in her nineties. Every time I saw her, I remembered the story Dad had told me about how she had run the electric company off with a shotgun when they'd tried to cut those trees down.

Bernice, looking fragile as paper, was surrounded by a small group of her relatives.

"Hi, Bernice! It's me, Blaine!" Dad yelled. I'm sure she was having no trouble hearing him. Nobody else was. I walked Trudy up next to him. Bernice looked at me through cloudy eyes.

"Here's Nancy!" Dad said. She smiled and raised a hand.

"Hey!" A familiar voice called, and I looked up to see an old schoolmate, Charlene Bucht, grinning at me. "You look good!" she said.

"Thanks! So do you!"

She started to say more, but I suddenly noticed Dad was gone. He had galloped off on Clifford and was in the parade again.

"Excuse me," I said. "I'm babysitting."

I turned and trotted after him. He appeared not to notice. People continued calling to him while he smiled, laughed and waved. "Hi Norm! Hi Frank! Max!"

Uncle Bob was standing with some of his family and he waved. "It's your turn next year!" I called to him.

When we rounded the corner and approached Aunt Connie's place, up by the school, Mom and Amanda and Rebecca started applauding and whooping. Aunt Connie's son James was snapping pictures.

The ambulance was creeping along behind us. A voice blasted over the loudspeaker, "Looks like you're the Grand Marshal, Blaine!"

Alan Hoey was laughing. "Blaine, you might be the oldest person to ever ride horseback in this parade."

"Oh. Thank you," said Dad. He looked sideways at me, winked and grinned.

As we made our way up the road, some tourists had a group of American flags that were snapping aggressively in the breeze. "Oh no," said Tess.

Clifford, who was in the lead, walked right past them. Trudy did a sidestep, and walked on then, but the rest of the horses refused, whirling and backing up. "Please grab those flags!" I heard Tess say. "Fold them up until we get by!" The tourists complied, and the group rode on.

The parade concluded at the baseball field, where all the races and contests would be held. There was already a crowd gathering, with crepe paper streaming through the grass and children laughing and dodging. The horses milled about for a moment, then everyone split up and rode off. Dad and I headed back down the road to our trailer.

I gave Trudy a neck scratch, "Good girl!" and jumped off.

I ran to help Dad dismount. As he took the saddle back to the truck, I grabbed Clifford and kissed his nose, and whispered, "Thank you."

CHAPTER TWENTY-THREE

What fell was relaxed,
Owl-downy, soft feminine feathers; but what
Soared: the fierce rush: the night-herons by the flooded river cried fear
at its rising
Before it was quite unsheathed from reality.
—From "Hurt Hawks", by Robison Jeffers (b. 1887)

I called him Frightful. He was named after a falcon in a book I had loved as a kid, "My Side of the Mountain", by Jean Craighead George. He wasn't a falcon; he was a broad-winged hawk, but he was truly frightful the way he would swoop down like a missile from the trees. He greeted me every morning as I drove out to camp, hunching in anticipation on the branch of an old birch. As the Revabus trundled along in a cloud of dust, he would come darting out ahead of it, breaking the air with his bent and spreading wings, pulsing with life, zigzagging beneath the heavy green canopy which hung over the dirt road.

The start of his tradition was abrupt, and he preceded me daily along that one mile-long strip of road. He would dip down low, almost touching the ground with his wingtips, then peel skyward again, and he zipped around every curve and twist along the way. I had no idea what could have motivated him to do this. I suspect he was a playful soul, and his soaring aerobatics were an indulgence in joy de vivre. It was nevertheless a glorious sight, and it made me feel privileged—no, *ordained*—to have such an escort.

At the end of his route, he would break off just as abruptly. He'd go swooping off to disappear among the trees west, across the road from the big rock and stumps that marked the entrance to Bernie Schmit's property.

I would smile and continue on out to camp, where Clifford waited to greet the dogs and me with a horrendous beller.

Frightful's summer marked the first year I remember of overwhelming tourism. Something had clicked, and Drummond was now the place to be. Both ferry boats were "running wild", crossing the river nonstop, packed with recreational vehicles that towed kayaks and four wheelers and jet skis and boats. Tourists came with their Ray-bans and golf bags and Bermuda shorts, bringing wives with perfect tans and designer clothes and paunchy bellies, and children in Sea World t-shirts. We locals had called these types "Fudgies" for generations. This was because they invariably hit Mackinac Island on the way up, coming away with many pounds of Ryba's fudge in assorted flavors, maple and chocolate walnut and white chocolate, all boxed in thin white cardboard that was stacked and held together with rubber bands. They always seemed able to ferret out a local, no matter how we dressed, and always wanted to know how big the Island was, what the population was, and if Tom Monaghan really owned the whole thing. They always asked for directions to the Rock golf course, Woodmoor resort, or a good place to eat.

A fudgie approached me once as I was sitting in the Revabus, in the lineup waiting to board the boat. He said, "What is there to do over there on Drummond?"

I looked at him. I was conflicted. A lot of my relatives depended on the tourist trade, but he had caught me on a day when I just wasn't in the mood. I scratched my cheek and squinted through my windshield at the royal blue St. Mary's River. "Oh, let's see. The hot air balloon rides are a lot of fun. There used to be a petting zoo, but the coyotes came and ate all the little animals. We still have a porcupine festival every summer, though."

He mumbled something, got in his car, turned around and drove away. He never did get on the boat.

Of course, I had lied about everything. We don't even *have* porcupines on the Island. As a rule, though, I tried to be polite and answer questions truthfully. I maintained a "live and let live" policy.

But then came the morning at the Bear Track Inn.

Bruce and I had come in for breakfast, and the place was packed. Two frantic waitresses dashed about the crowded tables, filling coffee cups and balancing loaded platters of food on their hands and forearms. "I'll be right with you," one of them gasped as she ran past me.

"No hurry. Take your time."

I leaned back in my chair, glanced over at Bruce and grinned. "Guess we had best be prepared for a wait, eh?"

"Yeah, looks that way."

We sat and chatted for awhile. I played with my silverware. Finally, she came over to us and apologized. She was a thin, red-faced teenager with strands of wispy hair coming loose and hanging down around her ears.

"Busy, eh?" I said.

She rolled her eyes, "Oh, yes, it is just crazy in here!"

"Well, don't worry about us. We're local, we've got all day."

She nodded gratefully. We ordered breakfast, and she scurried away, tucking her note pad into the pocket of her apron.

I heard a man's voice behind me. "Hey, can I get some coffee, here?"

He went on, "This is the worst service I have ever seen."

I did not turn around, but glanced up at Bruce. His eyes slid to meet mine in a gesture that told me he knew what I was thinking. I said nothing.

"Terrible!" the voice said. "Hell, we might as well go back there and cook our own breakfast!"

The waitress came out and set two glasses of juice down on our table.

"How much longer is it going to be, Miss?" the voice said.

She looked over at him. "I'll go check your order, sir."

"Good."

She disappeared again.

Bruce and I sat and drank our juice and chatted. The waitress came out a little later and set an omelet down before me, and she served Bruce his pancakes. "Oh, I forgot the syrup! I'll be right back!"

"It's okay. I like jelly on my pancakes." As he reached for the stack of jellies in the center of the table, I smiled at him.

My omelet was hot, and it tasted good, with tart pieces of ham and smooth cheese and little bits of broccoli and onion.

"What is this? Whoa! What is this?" the voice behind me said.

The waitress paused, "Yes? Is something wrong?" She walked over to his table.

"Did you put cheese in this omelet?"

"I believe there is cheese in it, yes sir."

"I did not order cheese!"

"I'm sorry!"

"Whatever made you think I wanted cheese on this?"

I looked at Bruce. I could feel my face getting hot. He smiled. "Take it easy, there, champ," he said, reaching over to squeeze my arm.

"Well," the waitress stuttered. "I—I just assumed that omelets have cheese…"

"Oh, never assume! *Never* assume!"

I threw my fork down with a clatter, and pushed my plate away as the now crimson-faced waitress rushed past with the rejected cheese omelet.

"Can you believe this place?" the voice said.

At this, Bruce got up and pulled out his wallet. I leaned forward. "Give me a dollar."

"Why?"

"Please, just give me a dollar."

He peeled out a dollar bill and handed it to me as the waitress came back with a fresh omelet and squeaked out an apology.

"Well next time," the voice said. "You'll know better, won't you?"

The crowd was thinning by now, and she went over and sat at an empty table in the corner with her face in her hands. Bruce stood at the counter waiting to pay the bill. I got up and walked over to the waitress. She looked up. "Did you need something else?"

I put my hand on her back and leaned over and whispered, "Yes. Watch this."

I turned and for the first time saw the owner of the voice. He was blond, with glasses, probably in his late forties. He was seated with two women who were watching me intently, but he seemed oblivious to my approach. I strode up to him and slapped that dollar bill down in front of his plate.

"Wha—what's this?" he said.

"It's an extra tip for your waitress. She's earned it. Never assume that omelets *don't* have cheese!"

As I walked out, with Bruce at my heels, I heard the voice saying, "What was that all about?"

I had the feeling he asked that question a lot.

They weren't all bad, the visitors to our island, but it seemed that year we had our share of bad eggs. People came screaming past our campsite on dirt bikes, tearing up the road, raising dust and noise. They drove at alarming rates, despite our warning signs that said, "Caution, horses and dogs loose." I learned very quickly to keep Clifford and Trudy in the corral between noon and five, when traffic was the heaviest—and the fastest.

But every morning Frightful was there waiting, ready to greet me and play our game. Nothing appeared to have changed for him. "Come on!" he seemed to say. "We'll just go deeper into the woods!"

And I did. As Frightful dodged away among the cedars, the dogs and Clifford and I ventured farther back in along the snowmobile trails. It was rough going back there, far too rocky and muddy for a car, but fine for a sure-footed pony and some dogs. We rarely met a soul on our ventures. Rarely, that is, except for the souls of the wild creatures indigenous to

Drummond: the great blue heron, the whitetail deer, the red squirrel. Loons and ducks abound on the inland lakes and coves and inlets. The days were long and golden along the rocky shores and among the sharply pointed spruce and sparkling waters.

Coming back from such a ride one day, with Reva and Scorch panting happily along at Clifford's heels, I topped the hill that looked down over the sawmill. I didn't recognize the truck parked next to it. A group of men clustered around the giant blade, and as I drew closer I saw to my horror that one of them was jumping up and down on the conveyor.

"Boy, this thing is sturdy!" he huffed, as *wham, wham, wham*, his feet pounded on the ancient machinery.

I urged Clifford into a trot, and reined him up next to their vehicle. "Hey!"

One of them looked up and smiled. "What are you, the plantation owner?" The others hooted.

"That's right."

Immediately his demeanor changed. He approached me with his hands folded in an expression of contrition. "So how old is this mill?"

"It dates back to 1792."

"Really?"

"Yes. The French erected it when they set up an outpost here."

He looked at me, not sure whether to believe this.

"Then the Indians took over and started tying soldiers to that conveyor. They say it's haunted. Bad luck befalls those who touch it."

He smiled. "Does it still run?"

"Only during a full moon."

He smirked, shook his head. "Okay, well, thanks for the information. Come on boys, let's go get some lunch."

As they drove off, I made note of their license plate number and turned Clifford up the road. Dad had mentioned going out to see Uncle Warren. I urged Clifford into a gallop and the dogs followed. But about a mile up the road, halfway to Uncle Warren's cabin, we met Dad coming back. The jeep squeaked as he braked to a halt.

"You'd better go check the mill and make sure everything's okay, Dad."

"Oh? Why's that?"

"I caught some fudgies there. They were really messing around with stuff."

"You kicked em outta there, eh?"

"Yeah."

"Good girl. I'll go take a look. Oh, did you find that kestrel Uncle Warren left for you?"

"No. I haven't been to camp yet."

"He found it dead on the road. He thought you might like to see it. He put it on the picnic table."

"Oh, a little sparrow hawk, eh? Okay. Was it a male or female?"

"I don't know."

"All right."

He turned the jeep around and headed back toward the mill. Clifford and I took our time, wandering down the road smelling the air as the dogs jostled in the roadside ferns. Images of kestrels flooded my mind's eye. They were tiny, beautiful hawks with a hatch mark over each eye. The males were colorful, having slate blue heads and dusty orange breasts. The dead bird might be good to use as a drawing reference.

By the time I reached the sawmill, Dad had looked things over. "Everything's okay here."

I nodded and turned Clifford toward camp. "You know, that was nice of Uncle Warren to think of me, and leave the bird that way."

But the mottled form splayed out on the picnic table was not a kestrel. It was a much larger bird. I got off Clifford and slowly walked over to it.

He lay with wings spread, feathers clumped in death. His head was bent, his neck broken. My stomach twisted. *Oh no.*

Dad pulled up just then.

"Dad, where did you say Uncle Warren found this bird?"

"Out on the road, down in front of Bernie Schmit's place."

No.

I stood quietly for a moment, running my hands over the still-warm feathers, smoothing them. Dad looked at me. "Do you want to bury him here at camp?"

"Yes." *Let us bury him here, close to us, not far from his own territory but where he will be remembered.*

"I'll get the tractor. We'll bury him deep. That way no animal will dig him up."

***

I drove that evening down the strip of road that had belonged to Frightful, past Bernie's place, past the old birch, and it hit me that there would be no more escorts; that the road would remain as lonely and silent as it seemed tonight. I pictured the fierce bird zipping along, unknowingly blessing some other vehicle with his aerodynamic escort service, swooping down ever so close—too close—to the ground.

"They didn't even bother to move him off the road!" As a sudden flood of tears spilled down my face, I looked around at the darkening forest, feeling the hush of the trembling poplars. The huge boughs of ancient spruce and cedar dripped with cones, sagging under the weight of years. It seemed that even the trees were mourning.

CHAPTER TWENTY-FOUR

"One loyal friend is worth ten thousand relatives."
—Euripides, Greek playwrite

My folks were planning a big shindig on Drummond to celebrate 50 years of matrimony. It was the first time in thirteen years that all eight of us siblings were going to be together, and I wanted to make the best of it. I was planning to take the horses along in hopes of talking someone into going riding with me. After all, who could resist an October trail ride through the woods and along the rocky shores of Drummond Island?

My brother Ted had arrived from Phoenix and was going to take the six-hour trek North with us for the reunion. I gave Clifford and Trudy a bath the day before departure, and then covered them with sheets so they would stay clean. Ted was helping me load stuff the next morning. He had some experience with horses, having spent a little time with my sister Raechel's endurance Arabs. He watched while I led Clifford out of the barn, and turned him loose in the yard to graze.

"You should have seen Raechel's horse! When she came to do that endurance ride in Arizona, she brought her horse with her and put it in her back yard. It was bucking and racing around the yard! It was so cute." He was giggling at the memory.

I grinned. "Yeah, they sure do like to play sometimes."

We got the trailer hitched, and the tack loaded, and then I went into the barn to get Trudy. I led her out, and, like the perfect lady she was, she stepped right into the trailer. Clifford eyed us the whole time. I expected him to follow her, but to my surprise, he suddenly flung his head, gave a squeal, and shot, stiff-legged, straight into the air. He took off galloping, and disappeared around the corner of the house. The dogs followed him in hot pursuit.

Ted watched as Clifford came running by, full tilt, and then disappeared around the corner again. "What is he doing?"

"Just playing. Just like what we were talking about." I dumped a little grain into the trailer for Trudy, as Clifford made another pass. He woofed as he went by me. I stepped out in his path and waited as he came around the corner again. I pulled a peppermint out of my pocket. "Come here."

He trotted up to me, but jigged impatiently while I unwrapped the candy, and then took off again without waiting to take it. He kicked up his heels, squealed and disappeared again behind the house. The dogs followed him joyfully.

Suddenly, it hit me. He was going North! He knew he was going to the North woods, to see Grandpa and have pancakes and trail rides, and have lots of nieces and nephews to hug and kiss him, and show off his tricks! The ritual was always the same; the bath the day before, the sheets, then spending the night in the stall. Then the next morning, off into the trailer they went. He was behaving just like a big happy dog eager for a car trip.

I started laughing and couldn't stop. If ever an animal was expressing pure joy, it was that horse. Squealing, neighing, jumping and bucking— and he could not settle down enough to even take the candy.

I could do nothing but stand there and let him make three or four more circles around the house. He finally skidded to a stop in front of me, blowing, and allowed me to clip the lead rope on his halter. I led him to the open trailer door, and he literally *jumped* in.

"Wow," Ted said. "He sure isn't like Raechel's horses."

CHAPTER TWENTY-FIVE

"Courage easily finds its own eloquence."
—*Plautus, Roman playwrite*

"I really don't feel like walking tonight," Amanda said. She was watching me unhook Trudy after our cart ride. The shadows were lengthening, the birds growing quiet. With each puff of wind a few yellow leaves drifted to the ground.

"I know. I don't either." I brushed Trudy off, led her over to the corral gate and put her inside. Clifford waited anxiously while I broke off several flakes of hay and tossed them over the top rail.

The anniversary party had been a huge success, and all our brothers and sisters were gone only a few days later. Only Amanda and I remained. I took her for a cart ride one evening, and we drove along the roads and laughed and hashed over the events of the past week.

Having company was pretty exciting for her. She had graduated from school a couple of years prior, and now worked a part-time job at the Drummond Island Laundry and Linen Service. Dad had initiated the laundry service to employ developmentally disabled adults in the area, and his efforts had elicited a lot of community support. Thanks to a group effort, it was now a reality. But the work was seasonal, so Amanda worked fewer hours in the fall and winter.

When I could, I would get her to take walks with me. Amanda hated walking. She had bad knees and little ankles and tiny feet, and she was overweight. I knew it was hard for her, but I always asked her to do it anyway. Tonight I bribed her. "If you walk a half a mile with me, we can do something special tonight."

She grudgingly did the walk. As we were returning, I asked her what she would like to do. She paused, with her hands on her hips, breathing heavily. "I know," she said. "Let's go to the bar and pick up some guys and then ditch 'em."

I shrugged. "Sounds good to me."

We drove down to the Northwood, to find the parking lot crowded with trucks. "Hm, they're busy tonight. Lots of guys."

Most of the "Ferry Boys", as Amanda and I called them, were there. They were seated at a table together, drinking beer. We saw them nearly every day as we crossed the river. They would guide our vehicles onto the boat, usually making a point to tease us when they collected the fare. We had special names for all of them. "Cryin' Brian" was a big beefy bear hunter, but the emotional sort. "Sad Brad" was a blond Nordic god who never smiled. "Pal Hal" was always congenial. "Duane the Pain" was very sweet, but woe to any Fudgie who crossed him! "Scotty Body" was possibly the kindest of the lot. His name was a stroke of genius on Amanda's part, as he was about five foot three and rail thin. And then there was Wormy, with his own nickname, whom we didn't bother to rename for obvious reasons.

They hollered as we walked in. "Hey! Manda!"

She waved to her fans, and directed me to an empty table. "Have a Coke, Nancy. You earned it."

Duane looked over at us, nodded and smiled.

"Ooh, Duane the Pain is hot for you, girl!" I crowed.

"He has the good taste," she said, struggling out of her coat and knocking her wig askew in the process.

There was a folk singer there that night, or at least someone I took to be a folk singer. He had his guitar and amplifier set up along the wall below all the deer heads and mounted fish. As Amanda and I sipped our Cokes, the singer began strumming a familiar tune, which I recognized to be Eric Clapton's "Cocaine". But the lyrics quickly caught my attention. He was singing a different version, which went something like,

"If you wanna have hair, Hair everywhere, Rogaine!"

I turned and looked at Amanda, and shook my head. "Do you believe this?"

She watched the guy for a minute, and then with impeccable timing, when he called out "Rogaine", she lifted her wig and exposed her bald orb.

I let out an involuntary yelp. She grinned at me wickedly, replaced her wig and began bobbing her head and snapping her fingers.

"She's all right, she's all right, she's all riiiiight, *Rogaine!*"

Up again popped the wig. "Wahoo!" she yelled.

I put my hand up over my eyes. "I can't take you anywhere."

She laughed and kept bobbing until the song ended. The folks around us were absorbed in their own socializing. I thought they were no better off for the show they had just missed.

The waitress brought us two Cokes. Amanda's lips closed over her straw, but her eyes were flicking around the darkened bar. She lifted her head. "Hey! There's our cousin! Denny Bailey!"

"Where?"

"Behind you!" She pointed to a table near the bar. Denny was surrounded by a group of what looked like vacationing businessmen. He ran the Drummond Island Yacht Haven, having taken over for his father, Glen. It was an incredibly busy way of life, and Denny was a person who always seemed like he was double-parked. I often wondered about his health.

"I'm gonna go speak to him," Amanda said. She rose.

"Oh. Okay."

She circled the table and went up behind Denny, who was immersed in conversation. She placed her hands over his eyes and roared, "Guess who!"

"Who? Who could that be?" he said, smiling. She removed her hands and he turned. "Why, it's Amanda!"

I watched as he introduced her around. I sipped my Coke, surveying the bar. The guitar player had started another song, and was unsuccessfully trying to get the Ferry Boys to join in. They were laughing and joking among themselves. A couple of other people had come in; tourists, I suspected, and were seated in the far corner. The waitress hustled over to their table.

A long few minutes went by, and I looked back to see Amanda still talking and laughing with Denny. He had now completely turned his back on the businessmen, and was totally absorbed in what she was saying.

I smiled. He had the good taste.

CHAPTER TWENTY-SIX

"All you need in life is ignorance and confidence, and then success is sure."
—Mark Twain

"We don't know what to do," Gina said. "Our barn is full, we've got foals from the last three years and now our vet wants to give Zach back. We've got no place to put him. Will you take him?"

I had seen Zach once. He was a tall, pretty-headed bay gelding with a star. He was now four years old and had had no training to speak of. Plus, he'd had a few bad experiences. The thing I remembered the most distinctly about Zach was his eyes. They were large, deep brown, and gentle. They revealed a sort of pathetic soul, but, I thought, a kind one.

I had two Morgans and three stalls. I said yes.

Loading him was interesting. When I went to pick him up, he was standing out in the pasture. He quickly came up to us, and was easy to lead. But he wouldn't get in the trailer. It took his owner an hour to load him. I found myself wishing I'd had the sense to bring Clifford or Trudy along, to give him confidence. I thought it surely would have shortened the process.

Finally, he climbed into the trailer and as soon as the door closed behind him, a loud clattering and banging issued from inside. The whole trailer shook and rattled. I jumped into the Revabus and took off, thinking that once we got moving, he would have to concentrate on balancing and wouldn't have time to display his displeasure about the experience. When we got home an hour later and he backed out of the trailer, I discovered to my horror that he had cuts on his face, over each eye, and the blood had gushed down to his chin. He had slammed his head against the walls in his panic.

He was gentle and easy to lead, so I took him into the barn and cleaned him up. The bleeding had stopped, and the horse was much more content to be inside the barn. He had fresh shavings in his stall, which had been Joe's stall, and clean water and hay.

I had already decided to send Zach out for training, and lined someone up immediately. It was the same person who had taught Trudy to drive in only four weeks. Trudy, however, was a piece of cake to train. Sharon had never hitched her, but she had ground driven her in harness. Besides that, Trudy was the sort of horse who tried very hard to do everything right. She was sensible and always naturally good.

I wanted Zach to learn to pull a cart. I thought it would be really good for him; to have harness parts slapping against him, the shafts banging him, something squeaky and bumpy "chasing" him. If he could learn to pull a cart, then it would be pretty easy to start riding him.

Before sending him away, I kept him for about two weeks. I wanted to get to know him a little, and during that time I worked with him a bit. He was very goosey about his mouth. He didn't want it handled, and would jerk his head away.

"Oh no Zach," I said. "You can't do that. You have to wear a bit someday."

I began touching his mouth, clicking and treating (he learned to like peppermints too), and within a day I could stick my whole hand in his mouth, handling his gums and tongue.

He hated the cross ties. He would shift forward and backward, dancing in place and swinging his head, pulling on first one side, and then the other. I clicked and treated him during the moments when he would stop moving. Gradually, his quiet moments lengthened. He finally learned to put his head down and relax, and stand still while I brushed and talked to him.

He was extremely one-sided; terrified of longeing clockwise. I tried it with him several times, and though I was successful on a couple of occasions, twice he panicked and tore the line from my hands and ran away. I decided not to try this anymore; that I was too much a novice to fix the problem. He went off to the trainer's and spent the summer there, while I took Clifford and Trudy to Drummond.

On my way up north during one return trip, I stopped to pay the trainer, and he said, "That horse has a screw loose. I can't get him broke to harness. He is just too nutty."

By this time, Zach had already been there nearly three months.

"Can you try putting a saddle on him?"

"Sure."

"Okay, well, don't get hurt. I guess it doesn't matter if he can't be driven, but he needs to be broke." I figured all the daily handling Zach was getting would have been good for him, even if the harness training hadn't been a success.

When I came back in the fall, Zach was going under saddle. He was being trained to go Western, which was fine. I got on him and rode, and was astonished by the length and ease of his stride. He was wonderful!

I hauled him to a boarding stable and boarded him during the winter. They had an indoor arena, and I thought I would ride him regularly. But I wasn't disciplined, and I didn't go. The few times I did, Zach was unruly in the cold weather, bucking and jittery.

In the spring, I sent him back to the trainer. "I think he needs miles put on him," I said.

I left him up there for thirty days, and then went to see him. I was shocked by his appearance. He was bone thin, skin stretched over a rack of ribs. His coat was dirty and ragged. He was as complacent as ever, coming over to me and lowering his head to be petted.

"Oh, Zach, I am so sorry," I whispered.

I had the trainer bring him home immediately. He got off the trailer drenched in sweat. "I see he still doesn't like to travel," I said.

"You want him in here?" The trainer led him into the barn and put him in the stall. He removed the halter while Zach backed up against the wall and rolled his eyes.

"Thank you." I paid him and he left.

I busied myself around the house for awhile, and then thought Zach would have had time to finish his grain and would probably want to be out with Clifford and Trudy. When I walked into the stall with his halter, he wheeled around and kicked me, a solid thump on the leg.

"Hey!"

He softened, relaxing a bit. I spoke to him, and he lowered his head and allowed me to put his halter on. But I was very upset by his behavior. I had never been kicked by a horse before and didn't quite know what to do about it. I contacted Sharon Harper, Clifford and Trudy's breeder, and asked her what I should do.

"Put him out on the grass and let him be a horse," she said.

So I did. We had plenty of green pasture, and he rolled and played and galloped with the others. I fed him four small meals a day, and handled him daily. I stopped giving him grain, thinking it may be giving him too much excess energy. I fed him hay and pellets instead. I always put a halter on and led him in and out that way, rather than just releasing him through the Dutch door.

There were things I really liked about Zach. His ears wiggled whenever he drank water. His eyes were large and dark and kind. He was always the first one to stop grazing and come up to me in the pasture. Perhaps most appealing of all, he adored Reva. Whenever she came close enough, he would scrub her head and face with his tongue. I found myself wondering how a horse this sweet and mild had ever come to have such low self-esteem.

When in his stall, he had developed a bad habit of standing with his face pressed against the wall as I approached with the halter. It was a submissive pose, though sort of meek and dreading. It was very difficult to get the halter on him when he stood like that.

I decided to change it. I came in with the clicker one day; the first time I had used it since his return. I held the halter out. He stood with his face pressed nervously against the boards. I waited. Finally, when he saw nothing was happening, he moved his head and looked at me.

Click!

His ears jumped forward and his eyes lit up. He remembered that sound! It was a good sound! I tossed the treat into his bucket and he immediately crunched it.

It wasn't long before he was approaching the halter and inserting his head when I held it out. Then, the gates of self-confidence suddenly sprang open for him. He was learning things faster. He learned not to rush through the Dutch door when I opened it. He learned to let me clip his mane. He learned to target, touching a cone on the floor, to reinforce that he could make good things happen.

What a relief it had to be, to know that he had control over some things, that not every experience was a random source of pain. Expectations were clearer to him now, and results were pleasant.

I didn't know it would ever be possible, but with the help of the clicker, he relaxed and grew fat and became a normal Morgan.

If there is such a thing.

CHAPTER TWENTY-SEVEN

"O, Wind, if winter comes, can spring be far behind?"
—Percy Bysshe Shelley (1792-1822)

They said it was zero degrees in Lower Michigan that January day. My interpretation though, was, "Whew, it *is* cold out there! Whatever possessed me to ride today?"

Well, it *was* sunny. Besides, I was a bit of a cold weather snob, having grown up in the Upper Peninsula. I never took the Detroit weatherman's threats seriously in the winter.

I hadn't had Clifford out in awhile and had been riding sweet, reliable Trudy. The difference between them was palpable. He was nosy and always busy. I had Trudy's sleigh bells hanging on the wall by the cross ties, and of course he had to investigate those. His ears leapt forward with interest when they jingled.

Trudy raced out into the pasture after us, trying to keep up, neighing. Clifford at least knew better than to answer. He was friskier that day even than usual, but I did get him to stand still next to the mailbox so I could check it. Everything was bright, the breeze was biting and the sparkling snow squeaked beneath his hooves. The dogs were elated! Cajun, my gangly German shepherd pup, his brother Cavar, and Scorch wrestled and romped, and Reva was in seventh heaven, never taking her eyes off her beloved horse.

I realized the mistake that day of always letting Clifford gallop back up the long driveway to the house. I didn't want him doing that this time. I could just see us hitting a patch of ice and going head over heels. So I made him walk. Did he pitch a fit! Head tossing, pretend bucking, dancing sideways. I made him turn in a couple of circles and that didn't slow him down at all. So, we did leg yields. A giant S curve, back and forth, always facing south but walking sideways. He did beautiful leg yields, but was forced to concentrate, and so we did that all the way up the hill. By the time we got to the top, he was willing to put his head down and walk quietly back to the barn. Then when I took his bridle off, he stuck put his nose in my hair and blew soft warm breaths.

But he had a spark in his eye; he was always thinking. Before I put him in his stall, he reached over and gave those bells another little ring.

CHAPTER TWENTY-EIGHT

"Action is the only answer to conquer fear."
—Dr. Norman Vincent Peale

That spring, my friend Rhonda had gotten involved in team penning, and was encouraging me to try it out. There was a group near Milford that was getting together on weekends. Well, it *had* to be more fun with your own horse. I quickly harbored fantasies of Clifford's transformation from hunter to cow pony. I began using a hackamore (or bosal) and teaching him how to neck rein without a bit. We practiced by chasing the dogs. He was, as ever, a willing conspirator, getting into the spirit of things by pinning his ears and nudging the dogs threateningly. "Git along there, little dogie!"

I was thrilled by his enthusiasm. I couldn't wait for the next penning meeting; to put the little fourteen hand Morgan among the big-butted Quarter horses and paints that were so favored among penners. We'd show them! Clifford could gallop, spin and stop with the best of them!

One day I put the bosal on and decided to go for a ride down the road. We passed the field where the old Standardbred mare stood by her apple tree, then passed the field after hers that was usually empty—but today there were cows in it: Two big red and white Herefords. Clifford came to a dead stop in the road. Up popped his head. He blinked. What was this? A billboard? A dumpster? A stump? With wiggling ears?

The cow's white head came up from where it had been buried in the grass. Clifford decided that now was a good time to turn around and go home.

I couldn't believe it! How could this be? My future penning star was—*afraid of cattle!* Oh no, why hadn't I thought of this before? I'd owned this horse since he was two. He was eight now, and we had been through all kinds of things together. All kinds of things—except this!

"Well, Clifford," I said. "The only way to conquer this fear is to face it! Forward, there, old buddy!"

He took a couple of steps, and then stopped again. His nostrils were flaring. The cows, seeing us watching them, decided to approach and check us out. It was too much for poor Clifford, who decided to do a little sidepass directly away from them. I had read about the calming effect of a scratch on the withers, so I tried it, and when I touched him he nearly jumped out of his skin.

"It's okay," I said. "Admitting that you have a problem is the first step."

The cows gazed at us passively from behind the fence. I got down out of the saddle, and as soon as I stood next to him, Clifford's head dropped and he began chewing peacefully. A little urging was all it took to convince him to follow me over to the fence.

"Take a deep breath, Clifford. Imagine yourself in a peaceful green field."

The cows were curious. They came over and stuck their noses through the wire. Clifford hesitated, then lowered his muzzle for a sniff. To my surprise, one cow's long pink tongue came curling out and reached for Clifford's nose.

"Uh oh," I thought. "He's not going to appreciate that!"

But he liked it. I guess he had been kissed enough by the dogs to not be offended. He actually stood there and allowed the cow to bathe his snout quite thoroughly.

I let Clifford eat some of the tall grass that was growing there. It's normally a no-no among equestrians, but I just figured he deserved some kind of reward for overcoming this phobia.

I got on after a few minutes, and then the dogs followed as we trotted back up the road. Clifford blew some happy purring snorts, evidently feeling much better after our session. The cows gamboled alongside us a little. Then they stopped and watched as we headed for home. I appreciated their friendly demeanor, which no doubt had helped us through the intervention. It kinda made me glad that, earlier that day, I'd had the veggie burger for lunch.

CHAPTER TWENTY-NINE

"A little of what you fancy does you good."
—Marie Lloyd (1870-1921)

The colors were vivid; bright early greens, blazing yellow forsythia and daffodils, and a blue spring sky. All seemed brighter from the back of a horse, I thought, glancing down at Clifford's chestnut withers. He plodded along in the sun, chomping thoughtfully on his curb bit. The dogs trotted, businesslike, stopping to investigate the roadside grass here and there, hoping to scare up a rabbit or pheasant.

A car appeared on the hill ahead of us, so I nudged Clifford over. Like ducklings, all four dogs clustered around the horse until the car went by. When it passed, they matter-of-factly scattered out on the road again.

"When the heck did I teach them to do that?" I asked Clifford. "Or did you?"

He lowered his head crossly at Scorch, who had carelessly paused in front of us. Scorch scooted away as I heard another car approaching from behind. I turned to look, and sure enough, the dogs trotted back into formation: Reva on one side, Scorch on the other, and Cajun and Cavar behind. When the car passed, they again ambled off to do Dog Things.

I figured it had something to do with the Western tack. The "herd" instinct. I closed my eyes and imagined us out on the prairie, with the coyotes wailing in the distance. I wished I owned a hat to complete the picture. And some chaps. And a lariat. I could hardly wait to start that team penning!

We trotted up the hill toward home. Not proud, I grasped the saddle horn as Clifford, who had not yet mastered the Western jog, bounced me into the air. I looked around as we approached the house. Thanks to a lot of hard work and some creative budgeting, Reva Ridge had begun to evolve since we'd moved in. Baby pine and spruce trees were scattered everywhere, pushing up hopefully from the grass, where hints of green tinged the ground. The front yard now housed an optimistic maple tree and a young birch. The lonely boulders were offset by burning bushes, just budding now, but which later would turn a blazing red. Rock gardens would harbor lobelia and impatiens, which I planted each year to bloom all summer near the porch in shades of deep pink and soft pink and red. Spiderwort and bluebells surrounded a stone birdbath. Bluebirds and goldfinches lined the wire fence or flashed overhead. Most of the rolling empty land was now fenced pasture, stretching generously along the hillside where the horses played and grazed. With a little help from me, Bruce had put the acres of fencing in, imitating what Jeff and Bob had done the first year. Behind the house, on a slope near the young apple trees, was the new blue barn. On its east side was a shady overhang and three Dutch doors, each adorned with a white "X"—as I had requested, "just like Mr. Ed's house." The barn harbored three large stalls, and was bright and well ventilated.

Trudy was jealously waiting in her stall when we arrived. After Clifford had been put away, I got her out to give her some special attention. She stood happily in the cross ties as I rubbed the chaff of winter hair off her neck and withers. My mind was whirling with images of lariats and cowboy boots. I mused that both of these horses ought to be natural Western ponies, having been sired by the great Serendipity Aries B, who was famous for producing Western pleasure champions.

I got to thinking about all those old cowboy movies with Roy Rogers, and how he had always sung to Trigger.

"Of course!" I said. "That's what's missing! The music!"

I burst into song. "I looove you, Truuuu-dee! *Truu-deeeeee, dear!*"

The dogs, who now lay panting in the barn aisle, looked pained. It was difficult to tell what the horses thought. Trudy was rolling her eyes, but I might have been rubbing an itchy spot. Clifford just stood in his stall, looking sleepy.

When I finished Trudy's song, I started Clifford's.

"We can be proud, of B Proud you see, Swift as the wind, and noble is he. We call him Clif-ford! Clif-ford! He has a red mane! He has earned his name, He's running free! You and I, Clif-ford—"

His ears popped forward.

"Will ride on Drummond like thunder…"

Naturally, when singing about him, it was impossible not to watch him. His ears went back again, then one or the other moved as I sang.

"And will you, B Proud, Be proud of meeeee!"

I decided to start over.

"We call him Clif-ford!"

Up popped the ears.

"Clif-ford!'

The ears remained perked forward, until I started the other part. "He has a red mane…"

I sang the song three times, much to the chagrin of the dogs. Each time Clifford heard his name, his ears would jump forward.

I remembered Roy Rogers saying at one point how Trigger loved music and singing. I wondered how he could tell. Now I know.

CHAPTER THIRTY

"My horse has a hoof like a striped agate
His fetlock is like a fine eagle plume
His legs are like lightning
My horse has a tail like a thin black cloud
the Holy Wind blows through his mane…"
—Navajo song

I was sitting at my desk, tap, tap tapping away at the computer when the monitor became a beacon. I looked around. The room was dark; very dark. I looked out the window and the sky had turned an eerie grayish-yellow color. Dr. Cawley was due to arrive in an hour for spring vaccinations, and the horses were out in the one pasture that had no access to the barn. I also realized the dogs hadn't been outside to relieve themselves in a couple of hours.

I leaped up and galloped downstairs to look for my shoes. *"Scorch!"* I was screaming. *"Get up!"*

The dogs roused themselves disinterestedly. I took down the baby gate and Cajun and Cavar came tearing out of the laundry room. I ran to the sliding door and pulled it open. The young dogs flew outside. Reva and Piper, the Papillon, meandered toward me.

"Come on! Come on!" I screeched, clapping my hands for emphasis.

We ran down the steps of the deck. The wind was beginning to pick up, and it felt cold. I flung open the basement door, closing it behind me, and let my "foster dog", Gus the rescued Corgi mix, out of his crate. He ran to the door and, thankfully, sat in front of it immediately, without being told, so I could open it right away.

We streaked across the back yard. Clifford nickered gently from the gate. I pulled the heavy barn door open and grabbed his halter and lead rope. He and Trudy waited patiently as I ran toward them and fumbled with the gate. Trudy stood like a lady while I put the halter on her. Zach waited respectfully in the background. The dogs raced happily in circles. Cajun was squealing hysterically with joy.

I pulled Trudy out and allowed Clifford to follow. He trotted off freely, and then paused to take a few bites of grass. The dogs circled him hoping for a race. Trudy and I headed for the barn as I glanced apprehensively at the west. The sky was gray and rumbly.

Trudy went calmly into her stall. I went in with her, taking off the halter while Clifford wandered in, checking things out in the aisle, and then went outside again.

I slid Trudy's door shut. "Clifford! Come on!"

Cajun shrieked in delight. Clifford's head popped in the door with a mouthful of green clover.

"Come *on!*" So he came in and walked into his stall. I rolled the door shut and quickly gave him and Trudy each a scoop of grain.

The wind blew, grumbling as I ran and grabbed Zach's halter. I could see him galloping back and forth along the fence line, frantic that he had been left behind. I ran to the gate. Rain began to pelt me. Cajun was wailing.

"*Shut up!*" I roared. Zach stood at the gate, jittery, eyes rolling. I tried to calm him then, lowering my voice to speak in soothing tones. He let me slip the halter on. I opened the gate. "Easy, easy."

He walked out, but his head was high, nervous. I thought Cajun's wailing was adding to his stress, and wished I'd locked him in the feed room. Zach wanted to run to the barn, but I made him walk. The dogs raced about madly, fueling his energy. Cajun was in hysterics. I told him again to *shut up!* We got almost halfway to the barn, and *bang!* A loud clap of thunder hit, and lightning zipped across the sky. Zach flew, all four feet, straight into the air, and began to run on the end of the lead line. Wonderful. Now was a great time to find out this horse had a storm phobia. I let the lead line play out to its full length as he circled me in a wild-eyed gallop. "Wup, wup," I said to him softly.

He slowed, coming in next to me again, looking fearfully around. The rain was pinging down on us. I walked him quickly to the barn. He tried to push past me into his stall. I made him wait, and I stepped in first. I was really proud of him for listening to me when he was obviously so worked up.

I got him into the stall, then I had to decide what to do. Should I leave his halter on or not? I had heard stories about halters on panicky horses getting caught on things, with disastrous results. But I didn't want to be struggling with a halter, on a scared 1000-lb beast, in a stall, when the sky could crash again at any second.

I decided to take it off. I left the door open a little behind me, whispering to him as I unhooked it, then I gently pulled it over his head.

Cajun was whining in the barn aisle. I flung the halter at him; it hit the floor and slid. *"You stupid dog!"* He ran out.

Then, it came, roaring like a freight train, a solid wave of rain. Cajun stood in the doorway, getting soaked, his ears sagging sadly to the sides.

I sighed. "Oh, get in here."

He transformed happily, galloping in, and began wrestling with Gus. Scorch followed me into the feed room, grinning. I glanced outside and saw Reva and Cavar standing out in the downpour. They had heard me screaming at Cajun and didn't know what kind of trouble was amiss. Piper, a little white blob, trotted aimlessly in circles, trying to decide if she should come in the barn and suffer the behemoths, or go sit on the front porch and get soaked. She finally opted for the porch.

"Reva!" She heard me above the din and came in. Cavar followed. I mixed Zach's feed. As I headed for his stall with the scoop, Scorch looked pointedly down at the floor by the big sliding door. He was right; the rain was coming in and puddling up. I pulled the heavy door shut,

thinking of Piper, and how Noah must have felt about those he was shutting out.

It roared, cracked and blew outside. The horses chewed their feed. I sang a song. Cajun and Gus kept wrestling. Scorch pranced around me happily. Clifford stood looking out his window at the storm.

Finally, it calmed. I slid the big barn door open and the dogs and I headed back to the house. I went in through the back door, and they followed with their muddy feet. The German shepherds, soggiest of the lot, were segregated to the laundry room while Gus and Scorch followed me through the house. I opened up the front door and there sat a sopping and disheveled Piper.

She streaked indignantly past my feet.

CHAPTER THIRTY-ONE

"Urge and urge and urge,
Always the procreant urge of the world."
—*From, "Song of Myself", by Walt Whitman (1819-92)*

Cajun von der Zalens was a tall, black and red German shepherd pup just reaching canine adolescence. It was clear that the hormones were kicking in; they manifested themselves in different ways. He would spend more time sniffing certain spots in the ground, and was becoming more attentive other dogs. I hadn't neutered him yet, as he had old and rare bloodlines that were of great interest to a breeder friend of mine. I planned to get his OFA certification when he was two years old, and then let her use him in her breeding program.

He was a big-jointed oaf, but generally a good boy. Things distracted him, and he was more highly motivated by his tennis ball than food. His favorite thing in life was to chase. He loved chasing anything—squirrels, frisbees, Scorch, anything that moved. I had to quickly put a stop to his sport of chasing horses.

Cajun's littermate, Cavar von der Zalens, was a pup I had rescued when he was four months old. The breeder had sold him to some people who kept him in a small pen with no shade and no water in ninety-degree heat. He was caged between two larger dogs who pulled his ears through the fence and chewed on them, until the tips were scarred and battered, as was his nose. One day I went to visit this pup see how similar he was to Cajun. I couldn't leave him in that situation. So I bought him.

Cavar was a shorter dog than Cajun, and lighter in color. He was stocky and well-muscled—the William Shatner of shepherds. Due to the size of his head and bone, I named him "Cavar", the Hebrew word for "big". I found that the word also meant "excavate", which was perfect too. Although he wasn't a digger, he had a strange affinity for shovels. Any shovel that came out would have Cavar standing right on top of it, resting his tongue on it, and jumping to pin it down if it moved. Cavar matured quickly and had taken to strutting around with his tail up, like a rooster. Both pups were blooming with youth and energy.

One day my sister Rebecca showed up with Jacob, now a precocious five-year-old. With them were Rebecca's friend Tracy, her nine-year-old son Shawn and T.J., his boxer.

T.J. was a round-headed dog, with bulging eyes and a cavernous grin, hot breath and a long wet tongue that flopped and rolled. Though T.J. was male, Cavar's infatuation was immediately apparent. I didn't know whether it was the boxer's svelte, thin waist, or the way his rump wiggled enticingly when he tried to wag his stump of a tail. But there was something about T.J. that Cavar clearly found irresistible. He circled the boxer, tail up, ears cocked back, and rested a paw on T.J.'s shoulder. T.J. flounced to the ground in a play bow, jerking his head from side to side in slobbery ecstasy.

I opened up the door and said, "Shawn, we've got that great big yard out there! Why don't you take Cavar and Caje and T.J. outside to play."

Shawn and Jacob obligingly took the dogs outside. I went to the refrigerator and pulled out some cokes. Bruce wandered over by the window. "Oh no!" he said suddenly.

He turned and ran through the door. I went to the window and looked out to the backyard. There was T.J., running desperately at full throttle, with Cajun and Cavar hot on his heels. Every now and then Cavar would leap up and grab him around the waist in a clumsy attempt at canine amour. T.J. was having none of it, galloping wildly in large circles. But the shepherds persisted with their attentions, Cavar finally grabbing and holding tightly, and Cajun grabbing him. Then the three appeared as one odd conjoined beast, a dog train loping through the grass.

The horses lined up at the fence and watched with great interest as Bruce gave chase, shouting something I couldn't quite hear. Bruce was stretched out, sprinting across the lawn, pumping the air with his fists, but despite their positioning, the dogs were much faster. I was vaguely aware of Tracy and Rebecca standing behind me, looking over my shoulder. Shawn and Jacob stood still, watching the spectacle, as Bruce, now flushed a deep crimson, turned to a tennis ball that was lying on the ground.

"Cajun! Here boy! Get the ball! Fetch!"

The dogs continued their ungainly parade as Bruce ran to the tennis ball, picked it up and threw it toward them. It plopped on the ground and rolled past them, unnoticed. Bruce turned to look up at me, calling my name, but then he saw that I was leaning helplessly against the window frame, holding my stomach in desperate hilarity as tears streamed down my face. He ran to the tennis ball, picked it up and threw it again, only to watch it fall and roll, a tiny, lonely sphere in the wide expanse of grass.

Just then Cavar slipped off T.J. and paused to whirl and snap at Cajun. Bruce leaped for him and grabbed him by the collar, leading him through the basement door. Cajun followed dejectedly. I heard the door slamming shut, and then Bruce's feet pounded up the stairs.

"That wasn't funny!" he said as he entered the kitchen. "How do you think seeing something like that will affect those kids?"

The front door burst open and Jacob came running in, out of breath and rosy with excitement. "That was *cool!*"

Shawn followed him, with a hand on the collar of the still-grinning T.J. "Wow," said Shawn. "I never knew dogs could run so fast on two legs."

CHAPTER THIRTY-TWO

"A heav'n on earth."
—*From, "Paradise Lost", by John Milton (1674)*

"What is your typical day like up on Drummond?" a friend asked me.

This is what I told her:

Days are magic. You wake up in the morning to the clean smell of northern Huron, and the gulls are screaming. The sun bursts through your window. The sky is bright. You can hear the chug of freighters on the St. Mary's River. You have breakfast; oatmeal or pancakes, and sit and listen while Dad tells stories. He might talk about his childhood, perhaps recounting one of the occasions when he fell through the ice, and how he got out. Or he might talk about what it was like in the old days, with colorful Island characters: Aunt Aldie who snared black bears and walked them into town on a rope. Or old Herman Adams who spit tobacco down his shirt front and kept chickens and a whitetail deer in his house. It's not so much the content of what Dad says, as the way he delivers it. His voice is a resounding baritone, but raises at times to an emphatic squeal. His steely blue eyes pop open dramatically, his crooked lips drawl out the words of whomever he is imitating. Even if it's the tenth time you've heard this story, or the hundredth, you laugh so hard it hurts.

After awhile you notice the clock. You throw some things together, get the dogs into the back of the truck and hurry to catch the ferry. If Dad is on the same boat, you get out and go sit in his truck, and laugh while he teases the Ferry Boys. The ferry might slow to grant right-of-way to a freighter, heading north to the Soo Locks and Lake Superior.

You watch as it passes, its bulk gliding along the river, tiny sailors leaning over the rail to look down at you. The ferry tosses and rolls in its wake. When the boat docks, you get back into your own vehicle, wave to whatever Ferry Boy is lowering the ramp, and then you drive off.

You drive along the long winding road, past Pigeon Cove, past Lyle Kelley's log cabin construction business, past Uncle Bob's house. Finally you roll into town, perhaps stopping at Sune's grocery for ice and pop, and some of the honey roasted peanuts Dad likes, and maybe some Snickers bars for Mom. You drive through the woods to camp, and are greeted by enthusiastic whinnies from Clifford and Trudy. You throw them some hay, let the dogs out and pump water.

You might help Dad then with whatever he is doing; clearing brush or building something. The chickadees hover around and you pause now and then to pull seeds out of your pocket and hold them out. After lunch you take a long walk, coaxing Lewis to come along. It's two miles to Reva's Lake. Scorch and Cavar and Cajun run races up the road and back, and crash through the thick stands of spruce, sniffing eagerly for squirrels. Reva walks by your side. You go up the hill through the deep, dark green cedars, dripping with needles, where the air smells like mud and balsam. You emerge at the quiet lake, where you see loons splashing and playing. You photograph tiger lilies and driftwood. The dogs drink and splash and chase the sticks you throw, and the loons swim closer to get a look at them. Your kingfisher blasts overhead. A heron takes off for the opposite shore.

You walk the two miles back home and maybe you have a cookout; eat whitefish or hamburgers for supper by the fire. Mom might have made potato salad that day. Your aunt and cousins may stop by, or some local friend or relative arrive to visit with Dad, or bring the kids to see the horses. You might bring Trudy out and give a couple of pony rides, and show off Clifford's tricks. The multitalented Scorch is always eager to do his tricks too; walking on three legs, falling down "dead", smiling and praying and a myriad of other behaviors.

As the shadows lengthen, company heads for home. You saddle up Clifford, and in the cool of the evening, back to the shore you go. The dogs trot along behind you. You get out to the open flat rock and work on your dressage moves; side passes and collected canter. Clifford is anxious to go, and he is all power underneath you, like a spring. On the rocky shore, maybe you see an otter or a doe and fawn, bolder now that the day is later. You leave Clifford by the dead cedar and throw sticks in for the dogs. The rock extends into the water like steps, and they plunge in and swim. You watch the sun going down, listen to the coyotes sing and the loons howl.

You get back on Clifford, and head for the road. A tourist blasts past you in a jeep, driving too fast, and you yell at him to go home. You get back to camp, untack your horse, feed your dogs, and throw the horses some hay before you lock up the camper and head back to the ferry. You might sit and visit with Amanda for awhile, maybe rent a movie or watch TV. It grows later, and you find yourself falling into a state of dimly flickering thought. Amanda looks at you knowingly as you grow quieter. Finally she laughs and says you'd better go to bed. Once you climb under the blankets, with Scorch cuddled up next to you unbeknownst to Mom, sleep comes almost instantly.

CHAPTER THIRTY-THREE

"There is no cure for curiosity."
—Ellen Parr (b. 1846)

I didn't know how many beaches there were left on Earth where you could turn horses loose. Every evening, when the shadows lengthened and the day cooled, I would saddle one Morgan and ride down the road with the other following, herded by three enthusiastic dogs. It's about a two-mile ride from camp to Clifford's Bay. The nice thing about going in the evening is that we didn't meet up with too many vehicles on the roads. The tourists had retired for dinner.

One Friday night it was Clifford's turn to run freely. It was always entertaining to watch him, because it was not just a graze-fest, it was a *party*. He liked to jump and buck and twirl, and attempt to get Trudy stirred up. That evening we rode along the ridge, down the very rocky and bumpy dirt road toward the bay. I enjoyed the sound of whispering poplar leaves, and the buzzing of evening cicadas. We were escorted for a short way by a very curious sharp-shinned hawk. He floated from tree to tree ahead of us, pausing to glare down at our strange caravan.

When finally the road curved out to expose the broad expanse of bright water, Clifford trotted down the trail ahead of us, tail whisking happily, and careened across the hard sand. He did a couple of spins, stopped, and dropped his head, then went down for a good healthy roll. The dogs, entranced, leaped about him. Trudy was intrigued by the campers across the creek, lining up to watch our entourage. She stiffened, her ears perked, and she blew an outraged snort.

I reached down and scratched her withers. "You're right. This beach is ours!"

We trotted around on the sand for awhile, then decided to cross the bay. The water level in Lake Huron was especially low that year. Trudy crossed to the shoal in the middle, and the dogs splashed after us. When Trudy stepped out of the water onto the shoal, she cast a glance back at Clifford, who stood defiantly on the shore as if to say, "I'm not getting *my* feet wet."

"Go get him," I said to Scorch, who was all too happy to comply. Followed by Cavar and Cajun, the lumbering German shepherd pups, he piled back across the water, splashing high, with bristling wet coat and growly barks. He and the young shepherds circled the little red gelding, yapping and dodging. Clifford just stood there, as if to say, "Is this the best you can do?"

Finally, Reva, then going on thirteen and nearly deaf and blind, caught wind of what was happening. She hitched her wobbly hind legs back across the cove, and when I heard her still-mighty bark, I knew it wouldn't be long. I wanted to get a photo of him crossing.

"Come on, Trudy."

We quickly entered the water, heading to the other side where it was belly-deep. Trudy splashed patiently as I fumbled with the camera, but as we stepped up on the shore, I heard a huge series of splashes behind us. I turned, and there was Clifford, galloping toward us, knocking sheets of golden water high above his head, and all four dogs swimming in his wake.

"Darn it!" I said. "I wasn't ready!"

He came out dripping and snorting, and then the group of campers approached us.

"Now *that's* an *Arab!*" One of them nodded toward Clifford.

She saw my confused expression, and added, "I saw how he had his tail up."

"Oh no. He's a Morgan. They both are."

She paused, frowning. "We have a Morgan, he's sixteen-two!"

I glanced over at Clifford, perhaps fourteen-one hands, from the back of little Trudy, probably thirteen-two. Their size had not even occurred to me as Clifford had been jumping through that water. "They are more like the old style."

The lady had a couple of little kids with her, and Clifford, after he had shaken himself, marched toward them.

"He's…Very friendly," I explained weakly, as by then he was purring snorts all over both little boys and the woman, too.

"Oh, my, yes," the woman said. "He's not like *my* Morgan. And the way he puts up with those dogs!" She nodded at Reva, who hovered at Clifford's side like a remora, scrutinizing his every move.

Just then, Clifford's ears perked forward with interest. One of the little boys was wearing nothing but a pair of very tight yellow swimming trunks.

"Uh oh," I thought. Clifford's head bobbed down, down, and he took a step closer to those trunks. His eyes had that intrigued gleam that always means trouble.

"Um," I started to say, and the kid, intimidated by the big head coming at him, took a step back and let out a wail.

Clifford followed him, and just as I was envisioning some truly awful things, Reva came to the rescue. She stepped between the boy and the horse, and her teeth clicked a warning in the air. Clifford, whose fixation on the yellow trunks was not to be deterred, began to sidle around her. But Reva snapped again, and he got the message. He went and found a tuft of grass to pull on, instead.

I heaved a sigh of relief. "Well," I said to the woman as I nudged Trudy. "It was nice to have met you."

As we moved off, the woman called, "Come back tomorrow! We'll have our cameras ready!"

I waved and smiled, but decided that she'd best stick to pictures of the kids with *her* Morgan. In those photos, undoubtedly, no one would be swinging through the air by their shorts.

CHAPTER THIRTY-FOUR

"To protect and to serve."
—Police Department motto

When Cavar was eighteen months old, I made the reluctant decision to find him a home. I'd had him neutered, hoping that would calm his restless spirit, but found that he still hungered for constant activity, and worse, he took his frustrations out on Cajun. Cajun's nose was covered with white hairs, healed scars from the bites of Cavar.

I had a friend who ran a German shepherd rescue group, so I called her and asked her if she had any suggestions. "Why don't you donate him to the police department?" she said. "They can always use good, high drive dogs like Cavar."

I called the number she gave me, and one warm September afternoon, Sergeant Edwards from the Detroit Police Department came to Reva Ridge. He was a big, friendly man with a big smile, and he put me at ease immediately. Cavar was an outgoing dog and went right to him. Sergeant Edwards got down on one knee and said softly, "Hi boy! Wanna catch bad guys? Huh?"

I liked how gentle he was with the dog, how he spoke, and his manner. He took out a tennis ball and threw it, and Cavar chased it happily. "I need to see what his drive is like," he explained. "So far, I like him. Now let's see if he will pick up other things."

He took out a PVC pipe wrapped in a towel. "This is what we hide drugs in," he said. "When the dog learns to play with this, we put drugs inside the pipe, and that's how they familiarize themselves with the smell of drugs, and eventually learn to search for them."

He tossed the pipe and Cavar brought it back. "Good boy! Good boy!" he laughed and patted the dog.

We played with Cavar for awhile. I showed him all the things Cavar had learned: Sit, down, stay, speak, shake hands, wait. Sergeant Edwards told me that if Cavar passed the training, and x-rays proved his hips and elbows to be sound, he would be assigned an officer and go to live with him in his home. They would be partners 24 hours a day. The training was all play, made fun for the dog, so he would want to work and be happy on the job. If by some chance Cavar didn't make the program, I would get him back.

Sergeant Edwards took Cavar after leaving me about six phone numbers by which I could reach him. He called me about three weeks later to tell me Cavar was doing fine, and to call him if I had any questions.

Months went by, and I did not call. Friends asked me how Cavar was doing. I did not know. I was a little afraid to ask, and just kept hoping that no news was good news.

Finally, one day in January I couldn't stand it any longer, and I called Sergeant Edwards. "Oh, hi!" His voice was happy, delighted. "You know, this is weird. I intended to call you today. Cavar is doing great. In fact, he's kind of a star."

I laughed. "I am not surprised, but happy to hear it!"

"Yes, he's due to graduate in February. I will get back to you with the exact date. Right now he's learning to search buildings."

"Does he have his partner yet?"

"Yes, he's been assigned a handler. It's a new handler, but has good instincts. And he loves the dog. I told him he was lucky to have that dog. I almost kept him for myself."

After we hung up, his words rang in my ears. "He loves the dog."

Cavar's graduation day came and my friend Carrie, who was the self-proclaimed Auntie to my dogs, had asked to come with me. Cajun had now matured to nearly ninety pounds, and I brought him along. He sat in the back seat and hung his head over my shoulder. Auntie Carrie squealed and hugged him. "He's a pretty bay-beeee! He's a *pretty* boy! Hi Precious! Hi, Beautiful!"

I ignored them both until Cajun tried to climb over the seat. "Get back there!" I roared.

"*Don't* yell at him! You'll hurt his widdow feewings!" Auntie Carrie twisted around to lean over the seat, stroking Cajun's broad head and cooing, "Your mommy is a big ol' meany."

I was squeezing the steering wheel, clenching my hands around it while my teeth clenched too. It was a two-hour ride to Detroit, and that was giving me plenty of time to work myself into a frenzy of anxiety. What would happen if, when I saw Cavar, he was thin and looked poorly? How would Cavar, who had grown up on a farm, adjust to city life? What would happen if I didn't like the person he'd been assigned to? Would I be able to reclaim him? I was worried that I had sent him down a one-way street and was dearly hoping I hadn't made a big mistake.

We pulled into the parking lot, past a chain link fence, and walked into the building where a bunch of uniformed police officers stood around. We were directed to a room upstairs, and there was a podium with a German shepherd logo on the front of it which read, "Detroit Police K-9 Unit."

Carrie and I sat and waited. We waited, and waited, and waited, as gradually other people filed in. My friends Ellen and Jan arrived, happily greeting me and chatting with Carrie and asking questions. I sat on the edge of my chair and twisted my hands together.

A little boy pointed to the logo on the podium. "That's Cavar!"

I looked up to see him sitting with a young couple and a little girl. I got up and went over to them. I indicated the little boy, who was watching me apprehensively with enormous brown eyes. "Did he say Cavar?"

"Yes," the young woman answered. "That's my brother's dog."

"Oh, okay. I raised that dog. Can you tell me how he's doing? Does he live with your brother? And how does he look? Do they get along?" I realized I was gabbling aimlessly but couldn't seem to stop myself.

She cast her husband a bewildered look. "We don't know. We've only seen him in his crate in the back of Rob's truck."

"Oh," I said, and then perhaps somewhat rudely, I returned to my seat. This was not good. Not good at all. Why had he not been introduced to the family? How come the family didn't know more about him? My stomach lurched in agony.

Then the officers and dogs filed in. "There he is!" Ellen said. She was right. Cavar moved brightly on the leash, grinning, his coat glowing with the sheen of good health. He was with a stocky young officer who was sort of a William Shatner-type himself. Cavar sat politely by his side with his back to us, facing the podium. They all were lined up, seven officers in dark blue uniforms with seven dogs sitting in heel position, and then a sergeant went up to the podium and began to speak.

"This is a group that has worked hard to be here," he said. "When they started out in this program, they could hardly walk these dogs without tripping over them."

I smacked a hand over my mouth to keep from roaring with nervous laughter.

"They have come a long way and have earned their place here today. The canine unit is an essential part of the police department. When we have a missing child or a bad guy that we need to find, the K-9 unit is called in. Then that dog takes us right to that child, or right to that bad guy. Then the handler packs them up in the truck and leaves. They are sort of like superheroes who come, do their job and then go, with no time for a show of thanks or appreciation."

"Nancy," Ellen whispered. "He's petting Cavar. Look."

I looked and sure enough, the young man's hand had wandered down to stray affectionately over the big dog's head, cradling it gently.

Cavar was turning, trying to see behind him, and sniffing the air. I had a feeling he knew I was in the room.

The officer at the podium said, "Let's have a moment of silence for those dogs who have lost their lives in the line of duty."

I looked around. Some of the officers were lowering their heads, some removing their hats. The room grew quiet except for the excited panting of the dogs. It began to dawn on me then, that this was serious business. These dogs were more than pets. They were true partners in a daily life-and-death effort. This was a show of admiration for them. This was respect.

A couple of other officers including Sergeant Edwards got up to say a few words, each praising the efforts of the handlers and the dedication of the dogs. Then, one by one, the officers and dogs marched up and received their certificates. When Cavar was called, it was announced that he was now a Patrol Dog. That meant he would sniff out narcotics, search for lost people, and do a variety of other duties. Carrie, Ellen, Jan and I whooped and yelled. The officers lined up with dogs sitting at heel, and faced us. We applauded wildly. I couldn't resist, and into the din, I called enticingly, "Clifford!"

Cavar's ears popped forward and he scanned the room eagerly, but he did not get up. He displayed the discipline of a true professional.

"Would any of the people who donated dogs like to say a few words?" the sergeant called.

Predictably, the people around me shrank back.

"I will!" I stood up and marched to the front. I stepped behind the podium having no idea what I was going to say, but figured I could wing it. A couple of jokes flickered through my mind, but then I saw the serious faces around me, the crisp uniforms, the absolute stillness, and I realized that this was a solemn occasion. I swallowed the urge to quip. "I rescued my dog when he was four months old from a place where he wasn't being treated right."

At the sound of my voice, Cavar's ears jumped forward again. He gazed up at me with a glowing, eager dog-smile. His rump, pressed tightly to the floor, wiggled happily, but he made no attempt to get up.

I grinned at him and couldn't resist squeaking, "Yes! It's me!" Then looking around at the serious faces, I said, "I already had his littermate and couldn't see leaving him there. So I bought him and brought him home. I then had two high-drive puppies, the same age, to contend with. I raised them but they were a handful and I didn't feel I could do right by both of them. So I decided to give one a life where he would have a full-time job to do. It was a hard choice, but it's so gratifying to come here today, to see them all in good condition, and know they are valued. I know I did the right thing. Thank you."

I stepped down and everyone applauded. I waited a little distance away while the group broke up, and Officer Rob took Cavar over to say hello to his little boy. As I waited, I saw Officer Rob's sister nudge him and point to me. Officer Rob turned, saw me standing there, and let the leash play out, and finally Cavar was allowed to run up to me. I fell to my knees, and as I gave that dog the hug I had been waiting six months to give him, tears rolled down my face. And there was Cavar, his broad furry head in my hands, his hard tail whipping against me; and Officer Rob was smiling, saying, "He's a great dog!" over and over, promising to stay in touch, and telling me he brushed Cavar's teeth and had his nails trimmed and bathed him in oatmeal shampoo and played ball with him every day; and other officers were coming over to thank me and tell me he was the best dog in the unit; and Sergeant Edwards was smiling down, telling me he had almost kept that dog for himself; and Carrie and Ellen were laughing and snapping pictures; and Cavar, my wonderful Officer Cavar, was leaning on me, giving me wet dog kisses, and crying with joy.

And it occurred to me that during my speech, I had left out the part that had surprised me. I had wanted Cavar to go to a place where he would be occupied and happy, and treated well. But in trying to do what was right for the dog, I hadn't considered how it was also right for the community. A rush of pride overcame me when it finally dawned on me that now Cavar would be the dog to find that missing child, or track down that bad guy. Now Cavar would be the superhero.

CHAPTER THIRTY-FIVE

"A horse gallops with his lungs, preservers with his heart,
and wins with his character."
— *Tesio*

Next door to Reva Ridge lived our notoriously cranky neighbor, Bob Donovan. He loved golf, and he maintained his twenty acres with precision, mowing constantly all summer. He had achieved a rolling green velvet hillside. The effect was most inviting to any equestrian, but of course I wouldn't dare succumb to the temptation. Our other neighbor, Ben Budlong, owned over a hundred acres of land, and he was right across the road from us, *and* he maintained a trail for me to ride on! What could be better? One September day he announced that there was a new path cleared, so I decided to take Zach over there. Zach at that point was still climbing up from his equine World of the Emotionally Warped.

Along on the ride came Reva, who was pushing thirteen, and nearly blind and deaf, but still Boss Dog. She lived to trail ride. Scorch and Cajun came along too.

The breeze was blowing and Zach was snorty and stepping right along, looking at everything pretty hard. As the trail wound along, Zach became more and more edgy. An old stove lurked with jaws of steel. A stump had two hollow eyes. A crooked log snaked along the dry creek bed. Branches rattled and leaves fluttered straight toward his skull.

This trail went on and on. The dogs were in their glory, rustling through the grass, unintentionally ambushing Zach now and then, except Reva who stayed right in her customary spot, beside the horse's right rear leg. Zach was jigging, wet with sweat, and his stress was tiring me out. I started wondering how far this was going to go; how many miles Ben had mowed of this one-way strip. I considered turning back, but we had come so far, and it just seemed as well to keep on going.

We came over a ridge where the path switched back along a fence line. I heard the drumming of hooves and looked up, and three fat horses careened up to us, blowing and bucking and squealing. It was too much for poor Zach. His rump tucked down underneath me and he shot forward, and then started spinning around and around. He straightened out, flung his head up and tried to gallop off down the trail. That didn't work, so then he thought perhaps reverse would. I finally talked him into completing his walk along the fence line, which he did, sidepassing the entire way.

By the time we got past the pasture, I looked back to see that Reva had disappeared. As alarming as this was, I was not about to turn Zach around to go look for her. I instead encouraged him to keep walking, and found a shortcut off the trail, via another neighbor's driveway. I did not have permission to ride on this driveway, much less with three dogs. But I was picturing Reva walking in circles, completely disoriented and lost in the woods. I cut down the driveway and then crossed the road.

The quickest access to my barn was across Bob Donovan's velvet green lawn. I did not have permission to ride across it. But I didn't hesitate. Zach jigged the whole way home, and I did not ask him to go any faster, not wanting to add fuel to his panic. Meanwhile, I was picturing Reva wandering off Ben's property onto the adjoining state hunting land.

I got back to the barn, whipping the saddle and bridle off the soaking Zach. I put him in his stall, and then opened up the barn door and called Clifford.

Ever curious, Clifford trotted in right away. I grabbed a bridle and saddle, and flung it on him, and then while I tightened the cinch, I said,

"Clifford, your dog is in trouble. If you can find her, you will earn a giant sized scoop of grain."

I decided the most practical thing to do would be to backtrack. So, off we went again, across Bob Donovan's pseudo golf course. Clifford stretched out and ran. I was picturing the flawless green turf flying up in clods behind us, and I cringed. I knew it was taboo, but; well, Reva was worth ten Bob Donovans. Clifford was wanting to play, and he ducked to the side when we went by a metal bin in the trees full of old garden hose. I told him to cut the crap, and that was the last of his goofing off.

Many horses will get nervous when the riders are tense, and that is what I expected. But Clifford surprised me. He stopped at the road, we looked both ways, and we led the dogs back down that driveway. We backtracked through the ditch where I had crossed. And we hurried. As we headed toward the trees, I said, "*Please* don't put me through that branch," and he went around the one that was pointed at my face.

The other horses were thrilled to see me arrive on yet another mount. I was scanning the field for Reva's body. We rounded a copse of trees, and there she stood, in the corner of the pasture, waiting for us. She was stressed and disoriented, but she'd had the good sense not to go wandering. Oh, what a relief it was to see her there! She saw Clifford coming and did not realize it was he; and she hustled to scramble out of the way. I jumped off and released Clifford, and he stood and waited for us, mowing grass. The other dogs were racing around, and when Reva saw them, she started smelling the air, searching for me. The wind was blowing scent all over the place. I went up to her and she dodged away from me. I had to squat down and call her, and then she seemed to say, "Oh! There you are!"

She came up to me and collapsed on the grass. She was all wet down the front from drooling. She was stress panting really hard. I hugged her and told her she was a good girl to wait for us. I said she was not going to go with that dumb ol' Zach any more. I hugged her and kissed her and just let her rest for a few minutes while Clifford munched, and the other dogs huffed and the neighbor's horses bullied around.

She walked home in her usual spot, at his right rear leg. Clifford walked all the way home very nicely and calmly, even across Donovan's golf course. We got back to the barn and Reva took a big drink of water. The other dogs flung themselves down in various places, panting happily. Zach bellered thunderously from his stall. Clifford rolled his eyes, silly and proud of himself. As I hugged and kissed him, Reva came over as is her custom, and sat before him to look up adoringly with her cloudy eyes. He bent down to her, as he always did, and blew gently on her face.

CHAPTER THIRTY-SIX

"Character is simply habit long continued."
—*Plutarch, Greek priest*

As I sat at my kitchen table working on a commissioned drawing, Reva lay stretched by my chair, staring bleakly at the wall. She heaved a big, bored sigh.

"Okay," I threw down my pencil. "Let's go. It's time to get the mail anyway."

The warm wind belied the season as we walked outside, with dead leaves scooting past and an autumn cast to the afternoon light. The horses raised their heads when they saw us coming, and ambled over to greet us. Clifford's hair was lengthening, the lines and cowlicks on his neck disappearing under the vigorous beginning of a winter coat. He thrust his nose eagerly into the purple halter I held out, and the dogs squealed in joy. They knew this gesture well.

He came quietly through the gate, but his head dropped so he could crop the grass aggressively. Looking out into the pasture, past the gate where Trudy and Zach stood in anticipation, I could see the brown earth laid bare in patches. Time to start giving hay.

We walked down to the barn and the dogs huffed in exultation as I tacked him up. His sides were bulging and warm, and he grunted as I tightened the girth. We started up the hill, and rode down the long driveway looking out over the fields. Bands of neglected pumpkins lined the furrowed earth; stripes of black and brilliant orange. Clifford's head was up and we trotted a little. He was anxious to go. I looked down, and there by his right hind leg was Reva, loping enthusiastically, forcing her wobbly hindquarters to move in a jerky rhythm. Her face was split into an ecstatic, old-dog grin.

We crossed the road to the farmer's field and Clifford could not resist an attempt to snatch at the mowed green turf beneath his hoofs. He knew better. I told him "no" and we moved on. Three fat horses were pastured there, and they galloped over to say hello. I humored them, letting them touch noses over the fence. The paint blew softly, and the pony wanted a turn, thrusting his teacup-sized nose into the greeting muzzles. Then along came the big, dark, Roman-nosed half-Morgan gelding. His mouth was open in a silent snarl and he thrust over the wire at Clifford's face. Clifford squealed, jerking back, but then wanted more. He seemed to think he could charm this crabby nag; after all, they must be related, however distantly.

"Nah," I told him. "Let's go."

So we left the others and followed the mowed trails through woods and fields. Clifford every so often tried to steal a bite of grass. I decided that his pasture must really be thinning. The dogs ran and swished through the piles of rustling leaves, flushing out birds and squirrels. Reva broke off to investigate some odor deep in the dead foliage, and then burst out to jauntily gallop after us.

We followed the trail and eventually emerged back onto the road, where we crossed and started home.

"Wait a second," I told Clifford. "I haven't checked the mail yet."

He had long been accustomed to standing still while I retrieved the mail, so that I didn't have to get down. But that day he walked up to the mailbox and tried to snatch at the tufts of grass below it.

"No!" I said.

His ears twitched back irritably. "Fine! Let's just get this over with," he seemed to say. He tossed his head, then reached over with his nose and flipped the mailbox open.

Chapter Thirty-Seven

"A source of innocent merriment."
—Sir William S. Gilbert (1836-1911)

"It's the darnedest thing, Dad," I said, glancing toward the window as I switched the phone to my other ear. "Thundersnow, they call it—when you have thunder and lightning in a snowstorm. I've never seen such a thing before. The horses have been coming in every night, and have been glad to do so, since it hit on Monday evening. But today, I think they are a little stallbound. I had put them outside all day with a bale of hay, but word has it we are getting six more inches. I don't know how wet the snow is going to be, so I decided to bring them in again."

"Well, bringing them in is easy," he said.

He was right. Each horse had a stall with a Dutch door to the outside. The doors were under an overhang, which provided shade or a nice shelter if their windows were open.

"How's that Clifford doing?" he asked.

I smiled. "Well, we had an incident when they came in today."

Being a creature of habit, I had developed a routine. The horses came inside in succession: First Clifford, then Trudy, then Zach. That day Zach walked up to his open stall door, looked in and then wandered away again. They had been eating hay all day long, and apparently the prospect of more hay inside wasn't worth entering for.

"Come on Zach," I crooned, but he ignored me, moseying over to Trudy's stall instead, blowing endearments to her over the Dutch door.

"Fine!" I stomped out of the barn, leaving his stall door open, and slammed Trudy's top door. Separated from his sweetheart, Zach ambled immediately to Clifford's stall to fraternize with him. I sighed in exasperation, stomped over to Clifford's stall and shut the door.

Immediately, the handle turned from the inside and Clifford pushed the door open again. It swung out suddenly and nearly hit me in the noggin. I had a clip that I could insert through the handle to lock it shut. I took the clip, shut the door and it popped immediately open again, exposing Clifford's leering horse face.

"Go away!" I waved a hand toward him. He flung his head and I slammed the door. I fumbled with the clip, the handle turned, the door swung violently open and there was Clifford, big as life and obviously pleased with himself.

Zach stood in the snow watching the proceedings with mild interest. The dogs romped and gamboled. I knew darn well the way to solve the problem was to go into Clifford's stall and give him some grain. That would keep him busy so that I could shut his stall door and coax Zach away from it. In fact, if I had grain, Zach would probably just follow me anyway.

But now it was war.

"Get back!" I said. So Clifford backed up. Quickly I slammed the door, and just as suddenly, it popped open. He looked at me. I looked at him. He rolled his eyes, thrust his head up and down, and shook his mane cheerfully.

I turned as if I was going to walk away. He watched me with interest. Suddenly I whirled, ran to the door, slammed it and fumbled with the clip. The handle began to move. Quickly I jammed the clip into place.

"*Aha!*" I shouted, jumping up and down in triumph. "I showed you, you bugger!"

The handle jiggled fruitlessly as I strutted back to Zach's stall. "Come on Zachie. Everyone's in. It's supposed to snow some more."

Cut off from his pals, Zach followed me quietly into his stall. The noise from Clifford's area had escalated to a rattling and banging now, as his door remained closed despite his efforts. I shut Zach's stall door and exited through the front of his stall and into the barn aisle.

"That's a good boy," I crooned to Zach. He began munching hay as I slid his stall door shut.

Clifford turned to face me as I moved up the aisle. "Herherherher," he said, swinging his head over the feed bucket.

I complied, giving all three horses some grain. I closed the big barn door behind me, then went into the paddock and undid the clip that held Clifford's Dutch door closed. He always liked to stand and look outside, no matter what the weather conditions were. The overhang offered good protection. But now he was busy with grain. Surely that took precedence over whatever could be happening out here, no matter how nosy the horse.

The dogs and I made our way back to the house, plowing through the waist-high drifts. Then I heard the unmistakable sound of Clifford's handle, turning again, and the rattle of the door as he shoved it open.

By the time I finished telling the story, Dad was laughing. "I guess he won that war after all."

"Yes, I suppose."

"That horse is one in a million!"

After we hung up, I thought about what he had said. "One in a million." That was a long way from "good for nothing". I realized that over the time he had spent with us, Clifford had proven to be many things:

A trail horse.

A rescuer.

A babysitter.

A parade horse.
A practical joker.
An ambassador.
A trick horse.
An explorer.
A fisherman.
A best friend.

And while I have learned a great deal from horses during my time with them, perhaps the most important is this: It is not what you achieve in life that matters. It is not the ribbons you win, nor your physical stature, nor the people you impress, nor the titles you earn. You can have all these things, and you can still be missing something. In the end, the one thing that truly matters is what is in your heart.

AFTERWORD

For more information on Morgan horses, contact:
The American Morgan Horse Association
122 Bostwick Road
Shelburne, VT 05482
(802) 985-4944
www.morganhorse.com

For more information on clicker training, contact:
Karen Pryor's clickertraining.com
1-800-47-CLICK
www.dontshootthedog.com

Be sure to read this wonderful novel by author

Nancy J. Bailey
Published by iUniverse

Holding the Ladder

"*A witty yet honest look at 'Starting Over'.*
Bailey explores the sudden imposition of tragedy,
which tests the bonds of true friendship.
HOLDING THE LADDER will remind you of the important things in life!"
—*Mikel Classen, Third Stone Publishing/Netbound Books*

Based on a true story, *Holding the Ladder* is a vivid, humorous tale about breaking away from unhealthy relationships and recovering from loss.

This luminous narrative begins with young Avery leaving an abusive boyfriend and moving to Arizona to start her life over. She is helped through the transition by her brother and his wife, a loyal dog, and three new friends. Through their support, a new romance, and the glimmer of a promising future, Avery begins to find herself again. Then one friend is tragically killed in an accident involving negligence. Subsequently, a breakdown in the group occurs. When the remaining two friends turn against her, Avery must find a way to cope with her feelings of grief and abandonment, and the implications of the accident. When she thinks all is lost, help comes to her in ways she never expected. Heartbreaking, warm and buoyant, this is an inspiring story of love and letting go, and the resilience of a woman's spirit.